'A beautiful blend of the poet ... fresh, soothing and helpful take on dealing with the ups and downs of life.'

Caroline Webb, author of How To Have A Good Day *and Senior Adviser to McKinsey & Company*

'This book is like a wise friend pulling you to one side in a loud room, saying just the right thing at the right time. The antidote to fake positivity, this pulls down the idea that "everyone else has it all together" (or that change has to happen overnight) and gives a real, kind take on approaching your next steps from where you are today.

An honest, uplifting, refreshing read.'

Marianne Cantwell, author of Be a Free Range Human

'Reading *Struggle* is like taking a deep breath. What a gift it is to have a reminder that there's a place beyond panic and fear, a place that might even hold new hope and potential. This is one to keep close on hard days.'

Josie George, author of A Still Life

'This is a book high up on the impact scale. It spoke to me as a leader, as a mother and as a human being trying to do their best and just not harnessing the opportunities which our struggles present. Empowering and energizing, practical and poignant, it's provided me a whole new perspective on life and work – all in Grace's warm and supportive coaching style. A book to enjoy and to keep close to hand to navigate the high and low roads ahead.'

Susan Clews, Chief Executive, Acas

'A helpful, thought-provoking book that you can either absorb cover to cover or dip in and out of when you need it. I am sure it will be a great support to people living and leading through 2021 and beyond.'

Kate Collins,
CEO, Teenage Cancer Trust

'In a world where resilience and coping are primary capabilities we look to develop, Grace has taken this subject and written this beautifully human, topical, funny, poignant and gripping read. Throughout the book Grace poses deep and revealing questions in to how as humans we deal with the uphills of life. This brilliantly written book opens up one's perspective on "what is a struggle" and "how best to deal with them" by sharing heartfelt moments we can all learn from. I feel lighter having read the book and would encourage anyone who is having to deal with the depths of despair that life can confront you with to give it a read.'

Steve Hurst,
VP Learning & Development, Sage

'Honest, relatable, wise and inspiring.'

Graham Allcott,
author of How to be a Productivity Ninja

'Living in chaos and uncertainty is our norm. This book not only gives you a huge hug and makes everything you are experiencing feel normal, it somehow manages to ground you, to anchor you to the moment and enable you through the many tips and topics to feel at ease with the struggle of it all. It gives you the courage to embrace the struggle and use it to your advantage to learn, experience and grow as a human.'

Caron Tickle, Learning and Development Leader, global science and technology company

'A practical and powerful meditation on struggle, Grace Marshall's book is an essential read for anyone who needs to get perspective on the value of life's tougher lessons.'

Bec Evans, co-founder of Prolifiko and author of How to Have a Happy Hustle

'Easily digestible and relatable. Grace takes our hand and guides us through the wild ride of emotions we all experience when we struggle, unpacking the negative associations and connecting us with the treasure that lies within the fight. Rather than something to be avoided, she helps us realize that embracing struggle can take us beyond just resilience, building the muscle we need to excel. With humour and down-to-earth reality, this is a highly relevant and topical reflection on the adage "strength through adversity" and, more importantly, how we can all find that strength within ourselves.'

Peter Docker, co-author of Find Your Why *and author of* Leading From the Jumpseat

'It's like having a life coach, but in a book, who you can choose to close the pages on (you won't!), and for a lot less money than actual coaching costs.

A compendium of dip-in-and-out questions to ask yourself no matter the stage of your "struggle", with a treasure trove of part funny, part emotional, fully gut-punching stories to help contextualize the snippets of Grace's wit and wisdom.

It landed on my lap during my own doldrums and I found gold between its pages.'

Katy Barnes, Head of Trading, Sky

'We all encounter struggles in our career. Grace Marshall helps you to get perspective in the tough times, to see struggles as opportunities for growth and gives you a firm but friendly kick into taking action.'

Helen Tupper, co-author of The Squiggly Career

'For years I subconsciously operated under the assumption that if something was hard, if it was a challenge, then I was doing it wrong. I had the erroneous idea that if I had the right approach then success would come almost effortlessly. Grace Marshall's book, *Struggle,* helped reveal these unexamined principles and showed me anew how wrong I was. This book will cause you to re-evaluate your relationship with obstacles and unexpected issues. Grace's soulful examination of our innermost insecurities will give you the confidence to say, "I'm not okay, and that's okay." It's better than okay... life's struggles offer humility, insights, and opportunities. The easy life is not only a myth, it's boring. A life of struggle reminds us that we are engaged in worthy pursuits and that we have what it takes to overcome.'

Jemar Tisby, CEO of The Witness Inc. and New York Times Bestselling Author of The Color of Compromise *and* How to Fight Racism

Struggle

The surprising truth, beauty and opportunity hidden
in life's shittier moments

GRACE MARSHALL

Practical Inspiration
Publishing

Contents

Introduction (or how I got here)

In a world that's obsessed with fast hacks, quick wins and Instagram perfection (cue *everything is awesome*), struggle has become taboo. A sign that something's gone horribly wrong.

But what if we've got it all wrong about getting it wrong?

As a Productivity Ninja (yes, that's an actual job title!), a lot of what I do is helping people overcome struggle. The struggle of overwhelm, distraction, procrastination. The struggle of working with other people, holding boundaries and setting expectations. The struggle of finding rest and rhythm in a world where work never ends. Much of this I wrote about in my last book, *How to be Really Productive*.

I am endlessly fascinated by not just how we work, but our relationship with work.

One thing we don't talk openly about in the world of productivity is the value of struggle. We speak of it in hushed tones with sideways glances, as an unfortunate affliction. Or we dismiss it irritably as an inconvenient necessity, a harsh reality to just get over. In fact, 'I'm struggling' is often seen as the opposite of being productive.

But I don't think that tells the whole story of struggle, or productivity. When productivity is just about getting things done, as quickly and efficiently as possible, we see struggle as an obstacle. A sign that either something's gone horribly wrong, or we are somehow not enough.

Not good enough. Not focused enough. Not driven enough. Not brilliant enough. Not clever enough. Not committed enough.

Struggle is a sign of failure. A bad omen. A wrong turn.
Or a battle, to face down, pistols ready at dawn.
A trap to be avoided or an enemy to be destroyed.

But what if it's not?

What if struggle is the partner, and the process, by which we discover?
What if struggle is how we stretch and strengthen?
What if struggle is not the obstacle to work – but precisely where the magic happens – where we do our best, most important work?

Whether you're wading in treacle, waiting for the storm to pass or just damn tired of the hustle, this book is for you.

Struggling? You're in the right place.

Who is this book for?

When I am asked this question, the answer is both obvious and ambiguous.

It's for the struggling of course.

We might think first of those who are vocal and visible in their struggle. Those in our networks who we know are struggling – at work, at home, with family, with ill health – those who are facing hard times, uncertainty, setbacks, demands, disappointments and difficulties. Those who are no stranger to struggle.

The jugglers and the scaffolders. Those who hold everything together. Who bear the weight of multiple commitments and know the reality of not having enough – enough time, enough resources, enough hands or headspace.

The swans whose kicks to stay afloat are becoming more obvious and frantic.

Those who are tired, battered or bruised by the storms of life. Those who are feeling lost, drowning in the double whammy of external uncertainty and internal anxiety.

But struggle is a universal experience. We may have different struggles, but we all know struggle.

So this is also a book for the soul-searching high-achievers. Those who have read and implemented every productivity book going, who are by all means successful, but know there is still something missing, unaddressed, niggling.

It's for the problem solvers who are no stranger to working hard and overcoming obstacles, yet find sitting and staying in struggle terrifying, unfamiliar territory.

For the seasoned leader, who wants to lead with more compassion and sustainability, to see their team thrive, who may have picked up this book primarily to help those around them, and may well find themselves in the pages.

And for the bright young thing, full of hopeful dreams, faced with setbacks, may this book give you the courage to take, as Chadwick Boseman put it, 'the harder way, the more complicated one, the one with more failures at first than successes, the one that's ultimately proven to have more victory, more glory'.[1]

Who is this book for? It's for the weight bearers and the fallen. For those who are brand new and those who are weathered. Those who hold it together and those who are falling apart. For those in between, and those who are both.

It's for you. It's for me. It's for us. We're an unlikely gathering, I know. Perhaps aptly not unlike an AA meeting. My hope is that in this space, in these pages, you will see yourself and you will see each other. And together we can learn and share with each other, and start living and telling a different story of struggle.

---

[1] Chadwick Boseman's Howard University 2018 Commencement Speech, 12 May 2018. Available from www.youtube.com/watch?v=RIHZypMyQ2s [accessed 17 November 2020].

PART ONE

Smarter

See the opportunity

What if we stopped seeing struggle as a battle
to fight or a problem to fix? Stop squeezing
and our world expands. We see opportunity,
not obstacle. This is the smarter way
to look at struggle.

When the shit hits the fan

Oh shit

When the shit hits the fan it's easy to jump straight into action mode.

Do something.
React.
Clean up.
Run away.
Fight.
Flight.

Even freeze is its own version of 'I should be doing something... but I'm not.'

But maybe Step 1 just needs to be 'Oh shit'.

Shit, that's not going to work.
Shit, it's all gone to pot.
Shit, what a mess.

Shit, I'm stuck.
Shit, I'm lost.
Shit, I'm out of my depth.

Shit, what just happened?
Shit, not this again.
Shit, this hurts.

Take some time.
Recognize the shit.

Before you ask 'Hey... what's going on?'

What is this shit?

Slow motion.
What's really going on here?

What looks like anger could actually be pain.
What looks like dismissive could be distracted.
What appears dangerous could just be different.

There are so many ways our brain misinterprets.

Our fast brain is inaccurate.[2] It is designed to find shortcuts, an efficient way of working. To do so, it fills in the blanks, pattern matches and jumps to conclusions. It looks for black and white. Good guy, bad guy. It thinks in contrast and caricature.

Our slow brain chews over and considers. It looks for shades and nuances. Examining angles, investigating puzzles, seeking and discovering...

What's really going on here?

---

[2] We don't actually have two brains. In his book, *Thinking Fast and Slow*, Daniel Kahneman describes two modes of thinking that our brain uses – System 1 (which I call fast brain here) and System 2 (aka slow brain). More about that later in 'Unintended superpowers'.

Fight, flight or...

Fight or flight. This is often our response to struggle.

There's an obstacle. Fight harder.
This is a bad place to be. Run away.

Fight

When we fight, we get the glory of the battle. The rush of the hustle. We dig our heels in, brace ourselves and say, 'bring it on'. Heart pumping, hyper-focused, we put on our armour and power on through.

Except all of this is unsustainable.

Beyond the initial push, when acute stress becomes chronic stress, our focus becomes single-minded and short-sighted. Our self-reliance becomes a silo, seeing other people as distractions at best, combatants at worst. 'It's up to me... Get out of my way... I have to do this myself...'

It's a lonely place to be.

Primed for battle, we start seeing battles everywhere. Expect a fight, pick a fight.

Our defensiveness shuts down our creativity. Fear and curiosity cannot exist in the same space. We see every opportunity as a risk. Every deviation as a liability.

We can run sprints in fighting mode, but we cannot run marathons. Nor can we build bridges.

Sometimes we break down barriers. Other times we just break down. We're not designed to fight all the time.

And when we get so used to fighting, we don't know how to enjoy the hard-won peace.

Flight

When we avoid the fight, we retreat. We stay safe, play small and opt for an easy life.

But that has its own costs. The cost of unfulfilled dreams, insecurity and isolation. If the danger comes closer, we retreat further, giving more ground, making our world – or ourselves – smaller. The things that lie on the other side of struggle become out of bounds.

Whenever we hit the dip, we divert and find a different path – we try a different route, unaware that success was just around the corner. Or we shut down, check out and cut ties, so that no one can come close enough to hurt us.

We get stuck in indecision and procrastination. We mistake the nerves of anticipation for a bad omen, a sign that we're not good enough. We disqualify ourselves – it's not for us. It's too hard. We relinquish our agency.

And, gradually, that 'easy life' carries its own burden: self-doubt, procrastination, indecision, self-disqualification. Better to spot your own inadequacies than have them pointed out to you, we think – except we find we are our own harshest critic. We swap the sting of disappointment for a dull ache of a nagging sense of unfulfillment.

A third way

What if there's a third way? Not so much a middle ground, perhaps more a wider ground.

Biologically, the fight-or-flight response gives us a narrow focus. In a life-threatening situation, we don't need a wide-angle perspective. We home in on the escape route or the weak spot in our enemy. We filter out what is possible and focus on what is necessary for immediate survival.

What happens when we stop fighting or fleeing? When we stay put and let the red mist subside, giving the rest of our brain a chance to catch up?

We start to pay attention.

We notice the treasure, the beauty, the opportunities. We lean into the discomfort and use its edges to refine us. We sift through the crap and find unusual treasures. We allow the compost to become the ground for new growth. We allow the grit to refine us.

Our limitations give us new perspective. Roadblocks redirect us down the untrodden path.

We widen our view.

We literally see more.
More possibility. More context. More nuances.

Beyond the options of fight and flight is a world of possibilities.

Where the unknown is not something to be fixed or avoided, but adventure to be explored.
Where being wrong is a doorway to discovery.
Where strength and power take many forms.

And emotions radiate beyond the black and white of fear and triumph into a whole palette of colour in between.

We ask better questions, beyond 'how do I defeat or escape this?' Questions of why and where and who and what if.

We see more than predator or prey – we see friend, traveller, lost child, teacher. And our roles are not limited to being successes and failures or heroes and villains but a whole cast of players, seekers, gardeners, makers, healers, wrestlers and embracers. Wild wanderers and steadfast stayers. Mountain movers and nest builders.

The land beyond victory and defeat is a land lush and deep, ravaging and wild, full of life in all its shades and forms. A land of caverns and creeks, glaciers and glens, rainforests and ravines.

And we as human beings remember that we are capable of so much more than running or fighting. We remember to learn, wonder, experiment, grow, digest, discover, create, repair, evolve...

What we see

Wrong turn, right where the magic is

In a world that celebrates the professional, the talented and the accomplished, it's natural to aspire to getting things right. And yet, many of life's successes and accomplishments are built on foundations of failure.

Thomas Edison found 10,000 ways not to make a light bulb, on the way to inventing the light bulb. J.K. Rowling hit rock bottom before writing Harry Potter, which was rejected 12 times. Bill Gates was a Harvard dropout. Albert Einstein could not speak fluently until the age of nine. Some of my favourite authors are ex-addicts.

Failure isn't an option. It's a necessity.

We often look at these examples and think they are a lesson in persistence and tenacity. They took lots of wrong turns before they found the right route. But what if that wrong turn is precisely where the magic is?

You see, our brains are lazy. We are biased to the familiar. Given the choice, we often stick to what we know. Until things go wrong, the temptation to keep doing what's still working is too strong a pull.

Innovation rarely comes from doing the same thing but better.

The inventor knows that creating something new requires deviation from the norm. The scientist in the lab knows that it's when something unpredictable happens that things get really interesting. The innovator knows that breakthrough lies in breaking the status quo.

This is fine when you're waiting for something to happen, to go wrong, to break through. But more often than not, the wrong turns come when we're not looking for it. They take us by surprise. They get in the way of the things we think we're creating or discovering or inventing.

The adhesive used in the humble post-it note was discovered by mistake in 1968, when 3M's Spencer Silver was trying to develop an ultra-strong adhesive for use in aircraft construction. The inkjet printer was invented when a Canon engineer accidentally rested his iron on his pen. And the idea for that beautifully mesmerizing toy, the Slinky, was born when naval engineer Richard James knocked over a spring intended for keeping sensitive ship equipment stabilized in rough seas.

What's getting in your way right now?

That detour you're having to take, that thing that's limiting, interrupting or irritating you.

What magic might be waiting to be unlocked?

Making mistakes normal

'We know we need to get more comfortable with making mistakes.'

I hear this a lot. Especially from organizations looking to become more agile, who know they need to take more risks, to innovate.

Except knowing it and doing it are always two different things.

What is it that makes it so hard for us to make mistakes? Or at least to make mistakes normal?

I made a mistake a little while ago, and didn't realize it until two weeks later. A client had made arrangements to come to an event and I realized I'd given her the wrong date. I left her a rapid voicemail hoping she hadn't set off, followed by an email. Eventually she got back to me – it was ok, she hadn't set off and could rearrange her plans to be available the next day.

As I stood on a train platform reflecting on how it felt, I felt a strange mix of exposure, vulnerability and gratefulness.

It was a silly mistake, a simple mistake, but one that caused someone else an inconvenience. When your job is to make your clients' lives better and their work more productive, a mistake that creates work for them can be sore!

Why do we hate making mistakes? Because we get punished.

Mistakes are rarely celebrated, and largely punished. Sometimes the punishment is small and subtle – a disapproving look, a sense of disappointment. Sometimes it's clear and set in stone – a fail, a fine, a freedom removed.

At the very least, a mistake costs us in time and resources, but more often it costs us in confidence, identity, position and belonging.

It's like getting it right is the point. And making mistakes is the deviation from that. Our society celebrates the professional, the accomplished. Not the learner.

The truth in mistakes is this: *It could have been better and I wanted it to be better*.

But the lie we often tell ourselves is: *I should have known better, done better, or been better*. In other words, *I'm not good enough*. 'That was stupid' becomes 'I am stupid'.

We confuse making mistakes with being a mistake.

A wrong note jars. But can also be the start of something new.

Deviations can lead to new creations. Falling short can give way to more connection when the other person reaches out to bridge the gap.

We learn so much more from when things go wrong than when things go right. But our tendency is to try and get it right without getting it wrong first. As Rachel Held Evans, quoting the poet Kathleen Norris, pointed out, we have a 'tendency to try and be holy without being human first'.[3] We're impatient; we look for shortcuts.

How human of us to try and avoid the human experience.

---

[3] Rachel Held Evans, *Inspired*, 2018, p. 109.

The lie that we need to fix, eliminate and avoid mistakes means that we never get comfortable with them. We never hold space or give ourselves space. We rush through, or beat ourselves up. We tell ourselves there's something inherently wrong about being in this space, which we then translate to meaning there's something wrong with us.

But when we don't engage with mistakes, we become really bad at making them. We deal with it in clumsy, knee-jerk, unhealthy ways. We shove it in a cupboard, let it fester, shift the blame or tear ourselves to pieces.

We fear mistakes because we fear rejection. We worry that getting things wrong will isolate and disconnect us; potentially get us kicked out from the tribe. And back in the days when we lived in tribes, being rejected was a case of life or death!

But my experience in this particular incident was the opposite. My vulnerability was met with understanding, and graciousness. My client and a colleague both stepped in to bridge the gap that had been left by my mistake. They helped to make it right. And they did so with a sense of shared understanding. They made space for my mistake.

It's a vulnerable place to be when you make a mistake. When you admit there's a chink, a breach, a gap where you fell short. But that gap is also a doorway. An opportunity for someone to step in, reach across and connect:

We know. Mistakes happen.
We see you; we won't look away.
We're with you. We'll figure it out together.
We'll stay and help clean up.
We get it; we make mistakes too.

What we see as a place of potential rejection turns out to be a place of connection. Of gratitude. Of community.

Perhaps we need to start celebrating mistakes, sharing them as open, normal and a sign of learning, growth and discovery. Bragging rights, anyone?

Take your time

Getting things wrong takes time. Doing what we know works is far easier, less painful and feels good, too!

Especially when we're busy. When we measure our productivity by doing things faster.

My husband is a seasoned software engineer. Junior developers often come to him with questions because they know he has the answer.

Given some time, they could probably work it out for themselves. Given space to play and fail and learn, they would develop the skills they need to find their own answers. But it's so much quicker to ask someone more experienced. So that's what they do. Because it's speed they're judged on as a measure of productivity, not growth, learning or innovation.

Sometimes my husband will sit with them and say, 'Talk me through it' and in articulating their thought process, they slow down enough to work out their own answers. Other times, he'll point them in the right direction without giving away the answer.

But he's under pressure himself. When he has requests pinging in left, right and centre, as well as his own deadlines to meet, it's tempting to reach for the quickest fix in the moment and just give the answer. Except, of course, that's precisely what perpetuates the pings!

So many organizations pay lip service to innovation and creativity, but in how they measure and reward productivity they stifle anything that doesn't look efficient.

When those who are praised and promoted are those who have a reputation for firefighting and responding to emails within nanoseconds, even when on holiday.

When our everyday conversations revolve around:

How fast can you get it done?
How soon can we deliver that?
Thanks for coming back to me so quickly.
Are we nearly there yet?

What we say is, 'What matters here is speed'.

We don't say, 'Don't take your time' but we do say, 'Hurry up'.
We don't say, 'Don't learn' but we do say, 'Is it done yet?'

It's in the everyday conversations that culture is set, and too often, we favour speed at the expense of mistake-making, risk-taking learning.

Perhaps it's time to steer our conversations more deliberately:

What are you learning?
Where are you developing?
What's new?

That thing that went wrong. That mistake. Tell me more about that. What do you notice?

How's the wrestling?
How's the wrangling?
Take your time; we're here to learn.

Crisis

When I was in my mid-twenties, I had my mid-life crisis. (I'm impatient – thought I'd get it over and done with early!)

I was working in an up-and-coming start-up full of over-achievers. The marketing department consisted of two of us: the marketing director, who made all of the decisions; and me, whose job it was to make it all happen.

I'd been a straight-A student all my life. 'Can do' was my middle name. I had honed the art of figuring out what people wanted from me and giving that to them. But the one thing that kept coming back to bite me was this: I needed to take more initiative.

The problem was, every time I took initiative and made my own decisions, I got it wrong. 'Why did you do that?' I'd get asked. 'Because I thought it's what you'd want me to do,' I answered, honestly. Taking initiative to me was nothing more than a guessing game. Figure out the right answer without being told. Turns out, of all the things I'm good at, mind reading was not one of them.

I kept getting it wrong. My confidence was chipped away in slabs. I ended up being sent on what I thought was a course for 'Better Decision Making', which turned out to be my first encounter with coaching. Instead of being told how to do my job better, he asked, 'What gets the best out of you?' 'When do you find yourself fully alive?' 'When does making decisions or taking initiative come so naturally to you?'

We explored things I hadn't thought of since my teenage years, when youth group discussions and my own introspective disposition led to lots of navel-gazing. Questions that circled around the fundamental questions of *Who am I? What am I doing here? What do I want?*

Long story short, I quit my job and started a family. My friends thought I was mad not to stay for the maternity pay, but I knew I had to cut and run. Once my baby came along, that's when the real identity crisis started. But from that came a slow journey of stripping away all the stuff I 'can do' and 'can be' and an excavation of who I am and choose to be.

I'm grateful to this day that I didn't work in a large corporate, where that gap could have gone unnoticed for years, shuffling from one department to the next, getting just enough right to survive being culled, but slowly, unassumingly, dying a little bit at a time.

It felt cutting being in that environment where there was nowhere to hide. But cutting, it turns out, was just what I needed.

In the early 15th century, the word *crisis* was a medical term. It was the 'decisive point in the progress of a disease... at which change must come, for better or worse'.[4] There's something cutting about a crisis. Something has to happen. For better or worse. Do or die.

A German term for mid-life crisis is *Torschlusspanik*, literally 'door-shut-panic', the fear of being on the wrong side of a closing gate.

---

[4] *Online Etymology Dictionary*, definition of 'crisis (n.)'. Available from www.etymonline.com/word/crisis [accessed 17 November 2020].

Crisis is the point in which a decision must be made – and therein lies the gift. There's no dithering, no sitting on the fence, no meandering, no being stuck in the middle. One way or another, something's gotta give.

It's often not until we get to crisis that we're willing to face difficult decisions, to get to the crux of what's really at stake.

When I'm working with clients coming to the brink of making an important decision, they often cycle around the sensible options first. They look for iterative changes and natural progression.

Go part-time instead of full-time, or two days instead of three. Negotiate the workload. Take some more holiday. This is instead of asking, 'What is it really about this role that's slowly killing me?'

Others will make big external changes – jumping from one job to another, starting yet another business idea, wiping the slate clean – only to find that, as the saying goes, wherever you go, there you are.

Often, it's not until you get to crisis point that you're willing to put everything on the table. This is where nothing is sacrosanct or set in stone, and everything is up for grabs. Only then do we really get to what matters (maybe it's the role, not the days) and what's possible (*what if I didn't have the title – would that give me even more freedom to do what I do?*).

As J.K. Rowling described in her Harvard commencement address:

> ... failure meant a stripping away of the inessential. I
> stopped pretending to myself that I was anything other
> than what I was, and began to direct all my energy
> into finishing the only work that mattered to me. Had

I really succeeded at anything else, I might never have found the determination to succeed in the one arena I believed I truly belonged. I was set free, because my greatest fear had been realised, and I was still alive, and I still had a daughter whom I adored, and I had an old typewriter and a big idea. And so rock bottom became the solid foundation on which I rebuilt my life.[5]

There's a clarity that comes from crisis, that doesn't come from natural progression. There's something in that cutting that cuts through the blindness of the status quo.

When things are too smooth, well-oiled and comfortable there's no impetus for change. We may tinker around the edges, but largely put up with things as they are.

Another way to look at crisis is the Greek word Kairos, which is used for describing significant momentous time, rather than Chronos, the linear, sequential time of minutes and seconds, which Olympian John K. Coyle describes as 'a special form of time magic where trajectories can be reset in seconds, and months of momentum can be released in moments'.[6]

Our experience of crisis is one of flux, uncertainty, and brokenness. That's why it's so scary. Things will break. But in that breaking lies a huge potential for change.

Or as Albert Einstein put it, 'In the middle of crisis lies opportunity.'

---

[5] *The Harvard Gazette*, 'Text of J.K. Rowling's speech', 5 June 2008. Available from https://news.harvard.edu/gazette/story/2008/06/text-of-j-k-rowling-speech [accessed 17 November 2020].

[6] John K. Coyle blog, 'How the Greeks hacked time: Kairos versus chronos', 25 November 2018. Available from www.theartofreallyliving.com/blog/2018/11/25/how-the-greeks-hacked-timenbspkairos-versus-chronos [accessed 17 November 2020].

Things will break. But in that breaking lies a huge potential for change.

Opportunity

When the status quo is well and truly disrupted, there is freedom to play, to explore, to experiment.

We found that when the Covid-19 pandemic hit. Things that were previously labelled as 'we can't do that' were now up for grabs.

For years, climate change activists and scientists have urged us to travel less, and we've said, 'We can't do that'. All of a sudden, the skies cleared, the roads quietened and oil prices dropped to negative.

Organizations that previously said 'we can't have our people working from home' discovered what's possible when everyone has to work from home. Hot-desking and open-plan offices gave way to remote and flexible working.

Night owls and teenagers across the world were free to experiment with sleeping and working to their own biological clocks, rather than the arbitrary nine to five.

Arbitrary measures of productivity like who looks busiest in the office could finally give way to a new definition of productivity, measured by impact and results rather than inputs and face time. (Although sadly it also gave way to a surge in employee monitoring software.)[7]

---

[7] Adam Satariano, 'How my boss monitors me while I work from home', *The New York Times*, 6 May 2020. Available from www.nytimes.com/2020/05/06/technology/employee-monitoring-work-from-home-virus.html [accessed 17 November 2020].

Businesses with disrupted supply chains reinvented how they deliver their products and services. Some found brand-new markets. Brands discovered that the real currency they had was in relationships.

And these innovations have happened faster than ever before.

Because when things are changing fast, when no one knows what they are doing, we can afford to do things imperfectly. Our collective tolerance for imperfection dramatically increases.

Innovation rarely comes from the core. It comes from the fringes.

Efficiency and experience value the core. The core is what we do well, what we've honed and refined and where we've forged our reputation. It's also where we are comfortable.

When the core serves us well, there's little incentive to stray away from it. Only when the conventional way is shut do we go to the fringes to look for another way. That's why it often takes a crisis for us to get truly creative.

When normal no longer exists, there is freedom to explore the crazy ideas.

And the way we innovate has changed too.

Online shopping, web-based yoga lessons, crowd-sourced film footage, virtual-reality house tours. Normally, these initiatives would take rounds of data analysis, market research, product testing, risk assessments and board approvals.

Even some large corporations which, according to *The Economist*, usually take a slow, expensive, insular, risk-averse and analysis-heavy approach to innovation, have been spurred into much faster, nimbler, collaborative and decentralized ways of innovating. According to Gary Hamel of the London Business

School, 'In a small crisis power moves to the centre.' But, he reflects, in a big crisis 'it moves to the periphery'. It may stay there for a while after the pandemic passes.[8]

[8] *The Economist*, 'The pandemic is liberating firms to experiment with radical new ideas', 25 April 2020. Available from www.economist.com/business/2020/04/25/the-pandemic-is-liberating-firms-to-experiment-with-radical-new-ideas [accessed 17 November 2020].

Impossible is a game changer

When the conventional way is shut, only then do we become open to the unconventional.

It takes a roadblock for us to seek a new route.

It takes constraints for us to explore new possibilities.

It takes a catalyst to create change.

Sometimes 'it can't be done' are the very words we need to hear, for something to rise in us.

That thing that's irritating you

When I think of learning experiences, I think of the big, the scary, the new and the risky. The times I need to step up or stretch outside my comfort zone. Times when I can see the learning coming and I can brace for impact.

What I don't think of are the curve balls. The lessons that crash land in the middle of just another ordinary day. These are the ones that leave me reeling afterwards with 'What the heck was that?!'

The ones that make me feel like I've just been punched in the face.

These are the ones I can easily miss as learning opportunities, because in these moments, I don't feel like learning. I feel frustrated, annoyed, let down and taken advantage of. I feel like retaliating, or retreating. Fight or flight. Blame or shame.

Who do they think they are?
What did I do to deserve that?

But these can be big learning moments.

My chemist friend, Jude, reminds me that a catalyst is essentially an irritant.

That thing that's irritating you right now – what if that could be a catalyst for change?

The gift of resentment

Most goal-setting courses tell you to set positive goals. Don't focus on what you don't want. Focus on what you do want.

Similarly, most marketing courses start with building your avatar. Your ideal customer in technicolour detail. Their name, their age, their family, what they read, where they work, what they care about, what keeps them awake at night. Confession: I have always been rubbish at doing this exercise; in fact, I often skip it!

Focusing on what you want helps to focus your actions. It's like my driving instructor said to me years ago – where your eyes go, your hands will follow.

And it's sound advice, once you know what you want.

When you're not sure what you want, when all you have is an inkling of an idea or a general direction, conjuring up some imagined fantasy is hard. And sometimes what we end up with is a stereotypical caricature of success, based on what other people have said over the years, of what a good job, or a good life, or a good client looks like.

In truth, my personal definition of success has grown incrementally over the years, with each decision, each project, each client. When something chimes well, I grow a little bolder and shine a little brighter. But when something jars, that sharpens my clarity like nothing else. That's when my understanding grows exponentially.

Woah, why did that encounter leave me feeling used?
What button just got pressed?
What boundary just got crossed?

When a client turns out to be a bad fit, or a partnership feels 'off'. When a tyre-kicker wastes my time or a supplier lets me down.

When something just doesn't feel right. And a voice within me goes 'Not this.'

It's the awkward encounters that have taught me the most – when I let them.

But let's face it, curve balls are time-consuming – in the moment and afterwards, when they play on our minds long after the deed is done.

When it feels like so much time has already been wasted, often the last thing we want to do is spend even more time on it. We itch for closure, either by lashing out or bottling up. But our quickest reactions can end up deepening the wound or prolonging the pain.

Learning from uncomfortable situations means sitting in that discomfort for a little longer. Riding out the grief or outrage until our considerate brain kicks back in and figures out something constructive to do.

Boundaries are a good example of this. Those of us who need to get better at holding boundaries rarely have this at the top of our to-do lists. As someone who's generally easy-going and accommodating, it's not until a line gets crossed that I realize where that line is.

The quick fix would be to write it down to 'some people just take the piss' or 'it's not you; it's them' and 'time to move on' – all of which has its place. But what I've found to be more helpful is to use the searing clarity of the experience to articulate my expectations and boundaries going forward and to be able to say more clearly – here's who I work with and how. Here's what you can expect of me, and what I expect of you. Here's what happens next. And no, you can't just buy me coffee to pick my brain.[9]

Resentment has a way of pushing its way to the surface. Sometimes it's sharp and jarring. Other times it wears you down slowly, but either way I've learned to pay attention to this particular kind of sandpaper. The stuff that rubs you raw can also be used to refine and clarify.

---

[9] Grace Marshall, 'Pick my brain: "Can I buy you a coffee" and other questions'. Available from https://grace-marshall.com/pickmybrain [accessed 17 November 2020].

Unlocking chaos

We often see chaos as something to control. When we struggle to contain it, tame it or fix it, we think we're doing it wrong. But what if we've missed the point?

We can't control the wild weather, but we can harness the energy of the wind and the waves to power our hospitals and homes.

We can't control toddlers (goodness knows we try) but we can see their energy and spirit as something to be nurtured and guided, rather than something to be tamed or subdued.

What if chaos isn't something to be conquered, but something to be unlocked? Untapped energy to be channelled, rather than subdued. Potential to be released rather than extinguished.

What if our job isn't to fix the chaos, but to reach in and bring forth transformation?

That's exactly what Elaine Halligan describes in her book *My Child's Different*,[10] which charts her parenting journey with her son Sam, who by the age of seven had been excluded from three schools, with a whole host of labels that earned him the nickname the Alphabet Kid.[11]

---

[10] Elaine Halligan, *My Child's Different: The Lessons Learned from one Family's Struggle to Unlock Their Son's Potential*, 2018.

[11] These labels included autism spectrum disorder (ASD), attention deficit hyperactivity disorder (ADHD), oppositional defiant disorder (ODD) and pathological demand avoidance (PDA).

In the early days, Elaine along with many schools and professionals, struggled to contain Sam's extreme behaviour: 'his quickness to anger, his impulsivity, his inability to focus and follow instructions, his distractibility and intense reactions to things that did not go his way'.[12] One school had been so unable to manage him they locked him in a cupboard. Another specialist facility advocated and employed physical restraint. The focus on containing, confining and controlling often made things worse, elevating his anxiety and his feeling out of control.

What turned the corner for them was learning positive parenting skills like descriptive praise, emotion coaching and positive discipline, which all focused on improving understanding, connection and self-esteem, in a way that helped Sam to understand himself, to take responsibility for his actions and learn from his mistakes.

Sam has since thrived into a confident, articulate, adventurous, independent, responsible and resilient young man, with an emotional intelligence and insight that is rare in someone his age. Reading and writing are still a struggle for him but that didn't stop him from graduating with a BSc in real estate management and becoming a serial entrepreneur running a classic car business repositioning cars globally.

As Elaine puts it:

> Sam is different. But now he owns this difference and he plays to his strengths. He has a drive and grit and resilience gained from all the experiences that shaped him. He suffered brutal failures in his early years, but is now making up for it tenfold, truly living life to the full.[13]

---

[12] Halligan, *My Child's Different*, p. 51.

[13] Halligan, *My Child's Different*, p. 164.

The guy who gets all the complaints

It's a hot summer's day in Waterloo station. Crowds are multiplying fast. Trains stuck on tracks, packed full with sweaty commuters going nowhere. The word *delayed* propagates across the boards, replacing times and estimates. Someone mentions something about fire on the lines.

In the middle of the concourse there is one guard, making eye contact with the crowd around him, responding to questions with the morsel of information he has, followed by a slight shake of the head as he openly admits that he shares their confusion, their uncertainty, their unknowing. He can offer no answers or solutions. Only presence.

It always fascinates me to see how people in customer-facing roles deal with complaints. Some get confrontational. They tackle complaints head on. In the heat and stress of the battle, they stand their ground, fight their corner, and argue 'It's not our fault.'

Some avoid it altogether. They disappear from sight. They turn off their Twitter feed. They bury their head in the sand until the whole thing's blown over. 'There's nothing we can do about it,' they reason.

But some take a third way.

They don't fight. They don't hide. They do something else entirely.

They show up. They embrace the situation – as an opportunity to help and to guide, to bring clarity or compassion, to restore peace, humour, sanity or dignity.

They don't see the struggle as a problem to solve, or a battle to fight. They see it as an opportunity to show up. To bring what they can to the situation. A sounding board, an understanding ear, a helping hand.

To do that, they need to let go of being right, of having all (or any) of the answers, and be willing to get stuck into the questions. Knowing full well that they may not be able to fix the problem, but they will be able to help.

These are the ones who build relationships and reputations. The companies that have even higher customer loyalty after something's gone wrong than when it was all plain sailing.

There is magic in the mess.
There is beauty in the chaos.
Struggle is the birthplace of
creativity.

Seeing within

The things we miss
when we rage

It shouldn't be like this. It shouldn't be this hard. I
shouldn't be struggling.

Sometimes our biggest struggle with struggle is the fact that
we're struggling.

Why is this so hard? Why am I still struggling with it? Why
can't I keep it all together?
Why me? Nothing's ever easy. Everyone's against me.
I can't believe this is happening again.

When we rage, it's tempting to over-identify and amplify our
emotions, and stray into what psychologist Martin Seligman
refers to as the 3Ps.[14]

We make it Personal: It's up to me. My burden. I have to do it
myself. Nobody can help me. It's my fault. I shouldn't be struggling. There's something wrong with me.

We make it Pervasive: It's not just this; it's everything. My house
is a tip, my garden's a mess, I don't see enough of my family or
my friends. I am meant to work part-time but have been working
full-time for months to try and keep on top of things. I haven't
taken a holiday in ages, I'm not sleeping well... I can't seem to
get anything right. Life is just one huge struggle.

We make it Permanent: It's always like this. I can't see an end
to it.

Anytime we find ourselves using the words, Always, Never, Everything and Nothing, the chances are we're raging. There's something very seductive about the certainty of black-and-white thinking. But it also makes the struggle worse and happens to be blatantly untrue.

When we get caught up in what 'should' be, we miss what is.

What's the truth here?
What am I actually dealing with?

These questions invite us to move from pervasive to specific. To examine and define the nature, size and scope of the thing we're dealing with. To see when it's there and when it's not there.

What is it that makes this thing so hard?
What is it that's behind this feeling?

Maybe you're dealing with lots of new things right now, and you've hit your limit for 'new things'. Maybe this feels particularly hard hitting because it's a matter close to your heart. Or maybe you're just damn tired and can't think straight, so everything looks worse right now.

What is it that I'm actually here to do? What's my role here?

When we get to the point where we feel like 'I just can't handle it,' it's good to ask what 'handling' even means. What is our role and remit in this situation? Is it really to ensure that nothing untoward ever happens, or is it to solve problems when it does? Is it to know all the answers, or to learn and develop? Is it to make it go away, or be there to support? To single-handedly save the day, or to work as part of a team?

What else is going on?

What is true, good or beautiful, in spite of (or even because of) the struggle? It's easy for the struggle to overshadow everything else, to see everything through the same lens.

I once spoke to someone who was so caught up in 'I have to do it myself,' that it wasn't until about 40 minutes into the conversation she found herself saying, 'I tell a lie. Someone did help me. I had completely forgotten about that!'

And therein lies the treasure. The support. The community. The fact that she wasn't on her own, and having help did not make her weak.

The things we miss when we rage are the treasure in the midst of the struggle. The spark, the smile, the glimmer of hope, strength, energy or purpose. The treasure that doesn't necessarily make the struggle go away, but changes something in you.

When we rage, we get emotional myopia. If something is bad, we can't see the possibility of good in the same space. If something's hard, we can't see how it can ever be easy. We can't see beyond what's right in front of us.

Just as George Orwell describes 'the great redeeming feature of poverty: the fact that it annihilates the future,' being in crisis mode makes you focus on the here and now.[15]

One corporate leader I worked with admitted, 'the problem is crisis is a very effective tool to get people to deliver. We're very good in a crisis so leaders keep using crisis to get people to deliver.'

---

[15] George Orwell, *Down and Out in Paris and London*, 1933.

In the short term, our fighting energy can be incredibly powerful. In the long term, we become adrenaline junkies, crashing from high to low and eventually burnout.

What do we miss when we rage? Here's the treasure:

The person who helped us. The person we become. The confidence or skill that we build. The knowledge that we can struggle. The overcoming. Or the surrender. It's all treasure.

And here's the work:

Adventures aren't meant to be predictable. Stretching isn't meant to be comfortable. Relationships aren't meant to be plain sailing. When we hit struggle, instead of thinking 'it shouldn't be this hard', let's start by thinking 'ah, here's the work'. Instead of thinking 'I've gone wrong', or 'I need this to end', let's roll our sleeves up and go 'this is where I need to be'.

The meaning we make

What does this mean?

That I'm failing or I'm growing?
That they're against me, or they're scared?
That I've gone wrong, or I'm right where I need to be?

Yes. And Yes.

It can mean whatever we decide it means.

Human beings are brilliant at creating meaning. It's what we do. From the ridiculous to the sublime, we weave story to create meaning and make sense of our experiences.

Perhaps a better question to ask is:

What am I making this to mean?

Noticing fear

'That sounds like panic...' said the counsellor.

I was blown away. Not in a million years would I have thought this seemingly articulate, cold, calculating, logical-sounding-yet-completely-unreasonable man was panicking.

My husband is an engineer. He is far more comfortable with logic and processes than people and emotion. He speaks fluent geek, and can see all sorts of things in code, but give him a WhatsApp group full of people trying to organize a car share, with names of parents and children being thrown around, and he's ready to tear his eyeballs out.

He also has a history of childhood trauma and unrecognized dyslexia, which means he has some well-honed defence mechanisms.

It's taken us some time to work them out, to notice when his defences have been triggered, and realize that his responses are to a whole lot more than what I have or haven't done in that moment.

Small events would trigger big reactions and deep hurt, which had me reeling between shame: 'How could I get it so wrong? There must be something wrong with me!' and blame: 'But all I did was... I don't deserve this! There's something wrong with him!'

And my typical emotional response in either case – to raise my voice, talk faster, getting more animated and expressive – all add to the panic and confusion for him.

What could he do if he could never express pain without me accusing him of overreacting? And what could I do if the smallest mistake or miscommunication could trigger a tsunami of pain?

When the idea of panic was put on the table, that changed everything.

What if he's not attacking me? What if he's panicking?

If I think I'm being accused, it's natural for me to want to defend myself. If I think I've been misunderstood, of course I want to set the record straight.

But if the person in front of me is having a panic attack, my go-to isn't to argue or justify or explain. It's simply to make that person feel safe.

Because until they do, there is absolutely no point talking about it. No point arguing with fear. Fear is not logical. Just as there's no point arguing with a toddler who is overwhelmed or over-tired. The best thing we can do is acknowledge their emotions and reassure them that they are safe. Eventually they find their way back (or fall asleep – as was often the case with my kids!).

What helps my husband to feel safe? Physical contact. A comforting hand. A reassuring voice. The last thing on my mind if I think I'm under attack, but the most natural response in the world if I think he's having a high-functioning panic attack.

Come to think of it, isn't fear behind most attacking behaviour, in work and in life? Where there's conflict, tension or stress, when we feel under attack or want to lash out ourselves – chances are, there's some fear lurking there.

I was on the receiving end of a colleague's email rage the other day (like road rage, but with email). It felt like we were at a complete impasse, until we started voicing our fears. Turns out, we were not at opposite sides of the same page. We were on completely different pages altogether, and our fears were largely unfounded.

So much can change when we learn to pay attention. When we notice fear, in ourselves, and in others. When we activate curiosity in the face of fear.

A better way of seeing

Fear says, 'Shit! Something's happening!'
Curiosity says, 'Oh! Something's happening!'

Fear says, 'Danger'.
Curiosity says, 'That's interesting!'

Fear says, 'Don't go there.'
Curiosity says, 'Let's take a closer look.'

Better questions to ask

What am I seeing? What am I not seeing?
What am I making this to mean?
What else could it mean?
What's great about this problem?

These are all questions that challenge our default to black-and-white, fight-or-flight thinking. Questions that invite us to look in between and upside down.

What-if questions are also great openers.

What if there's more to this?
What if that's fear talking?
What if this is precisely where I can do my best work?
What if this is a gift, or good information?
What if this is God or the Universe clearing my diary? What does this make space for?

What might be possible here and now, that wasn't before?

Seeing beyond

Find the treasure

We look for treasure in the obvious places. The shiny places. The halls, the palaces, the displays, the collections. Where the lighting is optimized and the air is sanitized.

We look there because that's where we like to keep our treasure. Neat and tidy, polished and on display. Accumulated and amassed to show off the best of our wealth. Curated, cut and edited.

We forget that this is never where treasure begins. Where we keep it is not where we found it.

Treasure is more often found buried in the dirt, lost in caves, or forged in fires.

When we forget that, all we see is the dirt, the dark, the difficulty, the pain and the loss. All we see is the shit in the shitty moments.

It's no wonder we want to check out. Checking out is our natural reaction to shit. Avoid it altogether if we can, but if not, do what we need to do to get through.

Minimal engagement. Minimal emotional investment. Hunker down. Shut people out. And just focus on getting to the other side.

Yet.

If we know that treasure can be found in shitty moments, we can recalibrate our radar. To pay attention. To notice the opportunity. To dig for the truth.

The truth may be that you don't have control over the bad news you have to deliver, but you do have control over how you deliver it.

The beauty may be in that one moment of human connection. The person who stops to ask how you're doing. Or sits with you, because that's the only thing they can do.

Treasure can even be found in the unreal.

Improv artist Karen Stobbe discovered when her father was diagnosed with Alzheimer's disease that the guidelines for improvisation were also helpful for being with a person with Alzheimer's.[16]

People with Alzheimer's often get told 'No'. No, that's not Betty. No, you never had a cat. No, it's not Tuesday, it's Friday. It's frustrating for them, and for those around them.

One of the principles of improv is to accept and build, using the words 'Yes, and'. Instead of correcting the other person, we accept their reality and go with the flow. Let ourselves be immersed in their world for a while, however wild and untrue it might be. In doing so, we allow it to be true for them, and we create precious connection on both sides.

[16] Karen Stobbe and Mondy Carter, 'Using improv to improve life with Alzheimer's', TEDMED talk, 2015. Available from www.tedmed.com/talks/show?id=526821 [accessed 17 November 2020].

Beyond binaries

Perhaps it's time to come away from pendulum thinking. From the idea that things are either good or bad. That people are either for us or against us. That we're either winning or losing.

My friend John is living with cancer. He chooses that term deliberately. Not fighting. Not beating.

Along with many others, he's fed up with the language of war that's often used around cancer.[17] It's not a battle that requires fighting. It's an illness that involves treatment.

Yes, 'let's beat cancer' is a strong image for charities and fund-raisers to rally support, but it can also be hurtful, when the phrase 'lost their battle with cancer' inadvertently implies that they didn't fight hard enough.

Besides, one of the biological effects of the fight/flight response is that our immune system shuts down (it doesn't help us fight or run away – it's not necessary for immediate survival), which is rather unhelpful if you really want your body to be focused on healing.

Pendulum thinking also results in swinging from one extreme to the next. Here's how John puts it:

---

[17] Simon Jenkins, 'Stop "fighting" cancer, and start treating it like any other illness', *The Guardian*, 28 January 2019. Available from www.theguardian.com/commentisfree/2019/jan/28/stop-fighting-cancer-ordinary-illness-language?fbclid=IwAR1xOBOxgAhKPwv_gbLuUCTro8EkmEfI-JbHFLOO4PFDTLWu-tNsSTurXy4 [accessed 17 November 2020].

Imagine a pendulum. One side is full-on depression about having cancer and the other is total acceptance of the situation without any worry, perhaps to the point where you can almost ignore that you have cancer.

You don't exist on one set point because you're not a robot; you have emotions and concerns that fluctuate depending on the latest scan or how you feel physically. Good days and bad days.

Going from one extreme to another is too large an emotional swing, sending your fight-or-flight stress system into overdrive. You've got to learn to accept the state of change and live in the middle with the tension it brings. Then it's ok to have a full-on depressive moment or an amazing euphoric day, because the swings are smaller.

This reminds me of a phrase I borrowed from a fellow mum, in the early days of parenthood: to be a good enough mum most of the time, with intermittent lapses into brilliance and hopelessness.

Here's an alternative: paradox thinking.

This thing is hard and exciting.
I'm in pain today and I'm also feeling good about…
I'm struggling and I am strong.
I know… and I'm also learning…
Things are good and bad.
It's a shitty situation and there is treasure.

And one of my favourites, a phrase coined by the author Glennon Doyle: Life is Brutiful – Brutal and Beautiful.

The contradiction of being human

Joy and sadness. Delight and grief. They are not mutually exclusive. They don't wait their turn. When they all tumble in at once they don't cancel each other out, but instead sharpen each other. The contrast they bring makes everything more vivid, more poignant, more real.

I messaged a friend recently to share that one of the things that makes me smile every time I see her in my social media news feed is our mutual friend Carol's smiley face in her profile picture. After the smile comes a wave of sadness and loss. Carol died three years ago.

But the smile always comes first. I can't look at that face and not smile. That's the impact Carol always had on people, so no wonder it's her legacy too.

If you're grieving today, grieve. If you're joyful, enjoy.

And if you're both, I'm with you. You're not mad. You're not weird.

Welcome to the contradiction of being human.

Holding your pain without feeding it

Holding painful feelings in a way that honours them but doesn't hurt anyone else is a very hard thing... I've learnt to feel it without feeding it, if that makes sense. It's a great, lumbering bear under my skin but I can hold it there calmly, making sure it doesn't bite anyone, until it goes to sleep again.

> Josie George (@porridgebrain), 25 February 2020, Tweet.[18]

There's a difference between feeling pain and feeding it.

Smarter struggle isn't about denying pain. It's about feeling it without feeding it.

Honouring it while holding it to the light. Not letting it crowd out everything else and take centre stage. Not blocking it out, and also not letting it block out.

Seeing it and seeing around it.

---

[18] Josie George, Twitter post, 25 February 2020. Available from https://twitter.com/porridgebrain/status/1232389241507926017 [accessed 17 November 2020].

Life, interrupted

'I'll do it when...'

When the kids get older. When work calms down or life gets less complicated. When I've caught up on my emails. When I've put out this fire, and the next. When we've recruited some more people. Or have more money in the bank. When I'm feeling more confident. Or less tired.

So often we see struggle as 'Life, interrupted.'

The obstacle that gets in the way. When things go wrong, putting life on hold, sending us into crisis mode, stopping us from getting on with the goal, the strategy, the vision, the life that we want to pursue.

What if *this is life*?

What if this shitty moment is precisely where life happens?

This is the life

What if, instead of waiting for the struggle to pass, we live out life in all its fullness – whatever the situation, wherever we find ourselves.

In the unlikely moments. The unexpected curveball. The shitty days, instead of waiting for the perfect day.

When we lead, even when we are not given the authority. When we show up, even when we don't have all the answers. When we speak hope, even when we feel crushed.

Life doesn't start when things are plain sailing. Life is in those moments of grappling, and wrestling. In the unexpected conversations, the detours, the dead ends.

Let's do it imperfectly, haltingly, awkwardly, but let's do it right here, right now, yes?

Unlikely leadership

Joseph was a confident kid. Some would say cocky. Full of enthusiasm, full of life. Beloved, a favourite in a family with a long history of favouritism. Loved by his father. Hated by his brothers.

He was going to be a leader. He was sure of it. Felt called to it.

Except life had other ideas.

Yes, he's the one with the multicoloured coat, the one who had the dreams... (*Ahahah*)

Joseph's journey to leadership was an unlikely one. Sure, he had a glittering start in life. Loved, blessed, bright and confident with a strong sense of purpose, calling and identity.

But then he gets thrown in a pit, left for dead, then sold into slavery by his jealous brothers. He gets it all taken away from him – his life, his family, his freedom – any hope of becoming a leader.

What would he have been thinking when he was stuck in that pit?

What kind of leader looks like this? Everyone hates me; who would follow me?
Look around: there's no way out, nowhere to go. Maybe I belong here?
Who am I, to think I could be a leader? Clearly I'm not good enough.
Maybe I got it wrong? Maybe I blew it?

When he arrives in Egypt, he rises in the ranks from slave boy to head of household, only to be falsely accused of rape by his master's wife when he rejects her advances. In prison, again he rises to leadership, sees a glimmer of hope of getting out, then gets forgotten for some years.

Twenty years after he was first sold into slavery, he ends up in Pharaoh's court, where he is put in charge of the whole kingdom, leading one of the most successful food bank programmes of all time, which sees an entire region saved from death, including his own family, when the story comes full circle and he is reunited with his brothers again.

If anyone qualified for *Life, Interrupted*, it was Joseph. And yet, he didn't wait for a better opportunity to come along, and he didn't abandon his dreams either.

Joseph's rise to leadership happens in the most unlikely of places. He lives out his calling, not in his own land, with his own people, but in a foreign land where he was sold into captivity, where he was a slave and where he was imprisoned.

And ironically, or perhaps aptly, dreams – the thing that got him into trouble in the first place – are the thing that gets him out.

What if this is life?

What if this shitty moment is precisely where life happens?

Small victories

Some days, winning isn't getting there or fixing that.
It's not getting to the end of the tunnel.

It's shining a light in the middle of the tunnel. Noticing one good thing, one step forward, one ray of sunshine in the middle of the torrent. One spark of beauty, however small or fleeting.

It's showing up. Doing the work. Not knowing if it's necessarily getting 'there' or knowing where 'there' even is, but trusting that each step, each stroke of movement, each whisper of a word, counts for something. And from those somethings, *Something* will emerge – a painting, a dance, a creation, a direction.

It's holding your integrity – or your temper – or your nerve. One breath at a time.

Activating curiosity, one question at a time.

Start small.

Start with one breath.
One question.
One helpful thought.
One action.

One spark of beauty, however small, however fleeting.
One act of kindness, of reassurance.

One moment of pause.
One prompt of 'Oh, that's interesting.'

Asking yourself, 'What is the best way for me to help you today?'

Giving yourself what you need, and letting it be enough.

It's astounding how often we overlook the things that work, because they seem too small. Too simple.

Someone else's shit

Before we move on, it's important to say this: not every problem is yours to solve.

When we care, when we are responsible for others, we can fall into the trap of becoming over responsible.

Your child's struggle at school is not yours. You may have your own struggle in how to parent them, support them and advocate for their needs, and that is linked, but it is not the same as the struggle that is theirs to feel and wrestle with.

As much as we would want to take it away, we don't do our best for them by taking it on ourselves.

The truth is sometimes when we let go of 'I have to solve this,' we can give better support.

My husband woke me up early the other day. He was in a rush to get to work, but couldn't find his coat, along with his car keys and wallet. I got up to help him, walking my way through the house, scanning, turning and searching as I went along. I found it in the end when I turned the light on in the orangery. While our hallway floor was being repaired, he had hung it up on a hanger in the window. In the dark, the black coat was perfectly camouflaged. Once the light went on, it was obvious.

What was interesting, I noticed, was that we were both doing the same thing, but having different experiences. He was stressed. I was not.

In his mind, he should be able to just get his coat and go. He needed to be out the door, to catch a train, and get to work on time. Looking for the coat was getting in the way of that.

In my mind, all I needed to do was to get up and help look. And I was doing that. If I had made myself over responsible for getting him to work on time, I would have been equally stressed and arguably less helpful.

What about the dog? (or why we panic buy toilet roll)

Someone once told me about a time when she worked on a support helpline for families of addicts. The situations they faced were pretty traumatic.

'He's taken the money. I can't afford to feed the kids.'

Then sometimes the call would take a surprising turn:

'But what's really getting to me is the dog.'

What would follow would be a vivid account of how the dog won't stop whining or the latest thing it's chewed through. Something tiny and inconsequential in the face of everything else, but this is what the caller would fixate on.

They referred to this internally as 'What about the dog?'

Similarly, when the Covid-19 pandemic broke out – a novel virus that most of us knew nothing about – people started panic buying, of all things, toilet roll.

'It's not even as if it's a stomach bug virus!' said my husband, echoing thousands of others who stared at empty supermarket aisles disbelievingly.

As bizarre as that sounds, maybe it's not that incomprehensible.

When we're overwhelmed by something we have little control over, we grapple for something we can control, that we can actually do something about. In the face of an unknown future

– and very much an unknown present – we go to what we do know. We fixate on something ridiculously inconsequential because it gives us the comfort of certainty.

I don't know how to keep myself or my family safe. I can't control the decisions made by the government, by my child's school or by my employer – but I can stock up on toilet roll and pasta. That I can do.

Of course, it was the panic buying itself that created a genuine nationwide toilet roll shortage. And isn't that how panic works?

How often does one person's busyness make those around them question if they're doing enough? How often do we hear 'I've got to...' and think 'maybe I should be doing that too?'

I wonder if there's something in our human instinct that grasps for the illusion of control, especially when we're faced with something overwhelmingly out of our control.

Clean the house. Research the health properties of olive oil. Or pick a fight over the washing up. Rather than confront the dysfunctional aspects of our family relationships.

Check emails. Say yes to meetings. Take on new projects. Be too busy to face the work that really matters – the work that scares the hell out of me.

Drink. Eat. Buy. Consume. Fixate. Help others. Find problems to solve.

What's your displacement drug of choice? Maybe it's not toilet roll for you. Maybe it's something else.

When we ran out of snacks in the house, and supermarket delivery slots were still an unknown rarity, I suggested that it may not be a bad thing for our kids to go without junk food for a while. My husband's immediate response was to order a bulk delivery from a discount sweets and snack shop! Not because he wanted to oppose me (although it felt like that at the time!), but because he hated the feeling of being restricted, of having choice taken away from him.

A few years ago, when my dad had his driving licence suspended while he was recovering from a brain aneurysm, and felt trapped and house-bound, he got into a massive row with my mum by insisting it was safe for him to go on a scuba-diving holiday.

There's something very innate in us that acts out when we feel out of control. When we feel we can't have something, we want it. Or more precisely, we want the feeling of control. Of self-efficacy. That we are in charge of our own destinies.

In the face of big questions that no one has answers to, we look for questions we can answer.

It's not about the dog. Or the toilet roll. It's about how uncomfortable we are with facing the unknown and the uncontrollable.

PART TWO

Braver

Trust the process

What if we stopped fearing struggle as a
wrong turn or a trap to avoid? We know we're
right where the magic is created. We trust
the process. We discover what's beyond the
safe and the familiar. This is the braver way to
journey through struggle.

When we're lost

End of the world as we know it

There's something about knowing that we associate deeply with competence, confidence and professionalism.

We turn to teachers because we want to know what they know. We follow leaders because we believe they know where they're going.
We give the work to those who know what they're doing.

We believe that our value, our professionalism, our expertise exists in what we know.
We are valued for what we know. We contribute what we know.

So what happens when we don't know?

When the path that lies ahead is uncertain, untrodden, unexplored?

When we don't know, we tell ourselves that something's gone horribly wrong. We become imposters, waiting to be found out. We're terrified to ask for help, because we believe we should know what we're doing. We feel the guilt of letting others down, because they trusted us to know.

In these situations, we flounder; we feel exposed, unqualified.

And yet...

When our job is to discover, to build, to create, to develop, then surely it's in the job description to go beyond what we know, and step into the unknown?

When our goal is to learn, surely it's not knowing that feeds our curiosity and signals 'here lies the treasure you seek'?

Those butterflies in your stomach – what if they're a good sign? An invitation to excitement rather than fear, a signal for adventure rather than foreboding?

In fact, it's only when we don't know that we're most likely to seek, listen, explore and learn. It's only when we stop relying on what we know that we become open to what's possible, new and surprising.

Somewhere along the line, we've mistaken certainty with confidence. We've learned to see unknowing as a sign that we're out of our depth, that we can't cope.

We think knowing qualifies us, and keeps us safe. But it also keeps us stagnant.

Curiosity, creativity and change cannot exist without unknowing.

Is the more capable person the one who never struggles or the one who knows how to struggle well? The one who faces struggle with vulnerability, courage and a willingness to learn, to fall, to screw up, to get up, to keep on showing up?

Great professionals know what they don't know. Dangerous health professionals are the ones who think they know it all.

A confident driver is one who recognizes the unpredictability of other drivers and road conditions. A dangerous driver is the one who thinks they are fully in control.

And when we're afraid of showing our unknowing because we don't want to let others down? Turns out owning our unknowing is the very thing that builds trust, as Brené Brown found in her research into courage and vulnerability in leadership:

> We asked a thousand leaders... what do your team members do that earns your trust? The most common answer: asking for help. When it comes to people who do not habitually ask for help, the leaders we polled explained that they would not delegate important work to them because the leaders did not trust that they would raise their hands and ask for help. Mind. Blown.[19]

The truth is, we're all on the brink of unknown territory. We live in an age of change, where uncertainty is the new normal, and the people we need around us – the people we need to be – are those who are willing to leave the safety of the known, and figure out how to live and work well in this new world we're getting to know.

---

[19] Brené Brown, *Dare to Lead: Brave Work. Tough Conversations. Whole Hearts*, 2018, p. 228.

Curiosity, creativity and change cannot exist without unknowing.

Into the unknown

Once we get over the initial panic that we've never been here before, we realize that actually we have been here many times.

The threshold of something new.
The doorway to discovery.
The beginning of a journey.
Being the novice, the apprentice, the adventurer, the pioneer.

We've been in new places before. We've done new things before.

We've been at this threshold many times before.
We know how to do new things, because we've done new things before. Many times.
We were born to learn, to discover, to explore the new.

Before we got used to what we know, we knew what it was like to not know.

Even in unprecedented times, we have our precedents, if we only remember to look.

The new normal

Something funny happens when you accept your reality as the new normal.

You stop waiting for it to pass.
You stop planning for when it's over.
You look it right in the eye.
You roll back your shoulders.
You rise to it.

You shift from 'How do I get through this?' to 'How do I want to live here?'

How do you want to live – not when this is over – but right here, right now?

Packing for the unknown

Years ago, when I'd pack for holidays, I'd always start with clothes. How many days would we be there? What activities are we likely to do? What kind of weather? I'd end up packing at least one outfit for each day, and then some contingencies. This top would go with that skirt, but also those trousers. But they'd need different shoes. Add a cardigan if it gets cold. Or maybe something waterproof. Except then again... different shoes!

Every time I'd come back with half of it unworn. The irony is, when I'm at home, I wear the same things all the time. But something about going away – about being somewhere unfamiliar – makes me think I need to be prepared for every eventuality.

It strikes me that we do this with more than clothes. We pack our bags with ready-made solutions. With answers. If this happens, I'll do this. If that happens, I've got this.

What if we packed our bags with questions?

Where am I?
What can I see?
What's safe?
What's exciting?
What's true?
What's beautiful?
What is my fear pointing to?
What is my curiosity drawn to?
What's going on out there?
What's going on in here?

What else could it be?
What happens if...?

Who do I want to be in this season?
What do I need to give myself?

Three questions

Three of my favourite questions come from a conversation with Martin, my church pastor, about Moses' encounter with God at the burning bush.

The story was a familiar one to me. It's the moment where God calls Moses to go to Egypt, and tell the Pharaoh to 'Let my people go' and lead them out of slavery.

At the heart of this encounter, Martin suggested, are three questions:

1. Where do you stand?

The question inferred is both literal, 'Take off your sandals, for you are standing on holy ground,' and metaphorical.[20]

As a baby, Moses was saved from decreed infanticide and adopted into Egyptian royalty. As a young man, he witnessed the oppression of his own people, and murdered an Egyptian in retaliation. When word got out, he fled for his life, spending what he thought would be the rest of his days living a shepherd's life in exile.

As an exiled criminal, Moses would seem an unlikely choice for a political champion, but he was also uniquely placed in his displacement, with the dual identity of the oppressed and the upbringing of the oppressor. Growing up in the royal court, he would have learned the culture, the political, societal and military systems and strategies of the Egyptians. It is from

---

[20] Exodus 3:5, *NLT*.

this place of displacement that God chooses him to confront Pharaoh and lead the Israelites out of slavery.

What's your current reality? What's the history that you stand on? Where are you now?

2. Where is your land?

This is the vision that God lays out for Moses. The exodus from Egypt, the rescue from oppression, the freedom from slavery. And the journey into the promised land, a land that is good and spacious, a land flowing with milk and honey, a land of plenty.

What's your vision? Where's your promised land?

3. What's in your hand?

In the story, this is the staff that Moses has in his hand – a common shepherd's tool – which God uses to perform miracles, by way of proof for those who needed it (Moses included).

For the rest of us, whether or not we believe in miracles or God, the question here is essentially, what do you have? What resources, skills or capacity do you have in your possession right now?

Where do you stand?
Where is your land?
What's in your hand?

So often we ask two out of three of these questions.

When we only know where we stand and where we want to go, we see the great chasm in between, all the resources, skills and capabilities we don't have – all the ways that we are not enough and don't qualify.

When we only see our land and what's in our hand, but fail to acknowledge where we stand right now, the plans remain as plans, unactioned, waiting for the perfect conditions to start.

And when we know where we stand and what's in our hand, but forget to look to the horizon, to set our sights on our land, we continue wandering round with our eyes cast downwards, dealing with the daily grind.

We need to ask all three questions together. That's when we get moving.

Feeling lost

We all have stories of feeling lost. That lurch in your stomach when you realize you're not where you're 'supposed' to be. When the places and faces around you are suddenly unfamiliar. When you lose your bearings, your anchor, or your destination.

I felt lost when as a child I took the wrong escalator at a metro station in Hong Kong, looked around and couldn't see my parents anywhere.

I felt lost when I moved schools in the final year of primary school, as the outsider, haunted by familiar sounds and smells (do all classrooms have the same smell?), in a sea of faces that offered no sign of friendship or familiarity.

I felt lost at university, surrounded by people with similar academic achievements and abilities to me, and I was no longer the socially awkward girl at the top of the class.

I felt lost when I wasn't the same. I felt lost when I was the same.

Funny that.

Feeling lost is unsettling. That's why we avoid it. We see it as a sign that something's gone wrong. Maybe with us.

Feeling lost made the Israelites crave the familiarity of slavery in Egypt. Desperate to avoid being lost, Hansel and Gretel collected stones and later breadcrumbs to lay a trail to lead them back to a home where their stepmother plotted to kill them. Perhaps it's also why some ex-prisoners reoffend and people stay in jobs they hate.

Better the devil you know, and all that.

Wilderness

Wilderness features throughout human storytelling.

It's where the Israelites wandered for forty years.
It's where Jesus was tempted.
It's where pretty much every hero and fairy-tale character winds up at some point in their story.

Wilderness is where people find themselves when they are lost. And it's also where they find themselves.

Stripped of our usual comforts, routines and pleasures. When nothing is familiar, we start to pay attention – really pay attention.

Is this food or poison? Is that shelter or a trap?
Is that thing keeping me grounded or weighing me down?

What do I think is essential? Who am I without that?
And even more basic than that, 'Where am I?'

When we lose our bearings, that's when we are forced to look, and listen. To the nagging thoughts, the yearnings, longings, the fears we push down and subdue, and distract ourselves from.

'The wilderness, by design, disorients,' writes Rachel Held Evans in *Inspired*, a book about journeying the wilderness of faith.

As any wilderness trekker past or present will tell
you, the wilderness has a way of forcing the point,
of bringing to the surface whatever fears, questions,
and struggles hide within. Nothing strips you down
to your essential humanity and inherent dependency
quite like submitting to the elements, surrendering to
the wild. In the wilderness, you find out what you are
made of and who your friends are. You are forced to
leave behind all the nonessentials, to quiet yourself and
listen.[21]

In our modern lives, we climb mountains, chase waves and
camp out under the stars, in a bid to retreat, to seek the
freedom of the wild, the expanse of nature.

But then we return, into the humdrum of commutes and
school runs, of habits and routines. Nothing changes. We've
had a brief escape, a little holiday. Now it's back to the grind.

Real wilderness is a transformative experience. It's an
encounter, a confrontation; you don't come out the same.

It doesn't look like picture postcards. It looks like terror in the
night. Feeling exposed, wondering if you've made a terrible
mistake. Coming face to face with your limitations and dependency. Surrendering the illusion of control.

We idealize the retreat. We think of the solitude, the freedom,
the get away from it all. But the power of a retreat is in the
irritation and the frustration. As Liz Gilbert puts it, 'Frustration is not an interruption of your process; frustration is the
process.'[22]

[21] Rachel Held Evans, *Inspired*, 2018, p. 49.

[22] Elizabeth Gilbert, *Big Magic: Creative Living Beyond Fear*, 2015, p. 149.

Frustration is when we're most likely to hanker for the old normal. But there's usually a reason we're in the wilderness. Normal wasn't working.

Ultimately, the question we ask in the wilderness is who am I?

Because it's not really about the wilderness. It's about the person in the wilderness. Who am I? What were my choices that brought me here? Who am I without this? Who do I choose to be stepping forward?

Feeling lost? Pay attention. Something's happening.

When we're stuck

Doldrums

I see you, restless.
Picking up one thing after another. Clicking between tabs, trying to find some focus, some momentum. They say crunch time is hard, but secretly you think this is harder. Being stuck in limbo. Drifting aimlessly.

You're not still. Nor are you moving.
You're restless, churning, static and stagnant.
You think of all the things you should be doing, could be doing, but that feels like a different place, a different time, a different you.

Give me time, a part of you says. *I need time*.
No, there's too much time, another part of you thinks. *I'm drowning in it*.

I find it fascinating that of all the dangers faced at sea, 18th-century sailors feared the doldrums the most. An equatorial region of the Atlantic Ocean where you could find yourself stuck in windless waters.

Not the raging storms or the treacherous ice, but the lack of activity, the lack of movement, the prospect of being stuck in nothingness.

Nothingness is deceptive.

Nothingness weighs heavy. It suffocates. It lulls you into an atrophy, a slow death.

I think it's the same with productivity.

What we struggle with – more than the overwhelm and the crises – are the doldrums, when we're in limbo. Rudderless and restless.

When the days are long and fragmented. When we never seem to stop working, and never seem to get anywhere.

When the pressure is on, it's breathtaking; it's bracing. This is different. This is a slow kind of atrophy. You worry that if you stay here much longer, you'll never move again.

And the nagging feeling that the rest of the world – out there – is moving. Out there, there is rhythm, and purpose, and a steady beat that's moving. Moving away from you, as you fall further behind.

I find limbo harder than all the states. Harder than back-against-the-wall deadlines, harder than firefighting, overwhelm, catch up or impossible juggling. Harder than complete switch off, hands off and letting go.

Limbo is exhausting in its own silent, creeping, insidious way. The more you stay there doing nothing, the more weary you feel.

Crunch time has focus and purpose. There may be panic over whether you'll get everything done in time, but there's no question of what those things are.

The doldrums rob us of both power and purpose. There is nothing we can do, and nothing to do.

Simultaneously, it robs us of rest. We're still occupied with activity. Some things still need tending to, so we can't stop entirely. And at any moment, the weather might change, when we'll need to be ready to hoist the sails again.

Which explains why so many of us have found living in a pandemic exhausting – even on days when nothing much is happening.

As a tweet that went viral put it:

> To live in a pandemic means to live with the constant hum of a threat. Somedays the hum might be so quiet it will lull you into thinking things are 'normal' and other moments it will roar back reminding you that while you might be done with it, it isn't done with us.[23]

It goes on to describe a 'sense of familiarity [that] soothes us into thinking we should "be back to normal" and when we're hit with fatigue again "Everyone else has it figured out, what is wrong with me? When will I snap out of it?"'

The lull is deceptive. The lack of something happening, coupled with the unease we feel, makes us think there's something wrong with us, rather than something wrong out there.

We're bored and on edge at the same time. Feeling like something's supposed to happen that's just beyond our grip.

Limbo is a place of in-between. Not quite here, not quite there.

The moments in between one stage of a project and the next. When you've just finished on a high, and then comes the waiting. When you've hit send on that email and you're waiting for a response.

The early days of parenting, or the summer after your GCSEs, when the days are impossibly long and the weeks are

---

[23] Sarah Noll Wilson, Twitter post, 25 June 2020. Available from https://twitter.com/sarahnollwilson/status/1276281247900356608 [accessed 17 November 2020].

hopelessly short. And yet. There are times when waiting is the work.

When nothing visible is happening, maybe something is happening. Something is brewing, fermenting, rumbling, transforming.

It's in the waiting that bread rises. And babies grow. And ideas germinate. And truth drops from head to heart.

It's in the liminal spaces – the in between – where transformation happens. Where one world ends and another begins. They are the places where creativity is born. Where bridges are built.

And just as it's in the fragmented conversations we have – on the playground, in the kitchen, in the car, at the water cooler – that we build relationships, maybe our best work is done in fragments, as we unpick beliefs and habits, and dismantle old systems thought by thought, word by word.

When it feels like you're going nowhere – maybe that's right where you need to be?

There are times when waiting is the work.

When it feels like you're going nowhere — maybe that's right where you need to be?

The things we see when we slow down

> On land, there is so much happening at once. At sea, your visual field is limited. Sea. Boat. Sky. Imagine seeing that for months. Your brain stops looking for constant stimulation and gets more attuned. What looks boring starts to become interesting.

These are the words of Martha, who was once becalmed at sea for 40 days.

What was just green becomes many shades of green. You notice the subtle differences in the formation of cloud, the sounds of the sea.

We see in more depth when we slow down. We notice the details. We become immersed in life, rather than racing through.

But that also means we feel more. Deeper. More vivid. More visceral. The cuts cut deeper. The lows swoop to inkier depths.

And there's a loss to that too.

Below deck

The thing about paying attention is that you notice everything.

Including the stuff you were successfully avoiding up until now. The stuff below deck.

For my friend Josie, who charts her life in the slow lane with chronic pain and disability in her memoir *A Still Life*, digging underneath the feeling of doldrums revealed a deeper truth lurking under the still waters. Here's what she told me in a text conversation:

> When I examine that feeling, I find a lot of fear but also a MASSIVE EGO! Fear of being left behind, fear of not being special, embarrassment and shame that my journey doesn't look different to this, that I can't be more visibly impressive, fear of becoming more and more invisible and what that translates about my worth, fear of disappearing, not measuring up, fear and doubt that I'm on the wrong path altogether...
>
> There is so much tied up in that restless uncomfortableness and often it's pinpointing its raw ugly truth that helps blow a breath of wind in my sails. 'Ah, I feel horrible because this is going to take a long time and I want to be special and impressive NOW.' It kind of pops the pressure bubble of it, and then I can look up and out and see that, actually, there is a little movement here, something I could chase if I could leave

my ego below deck, and that it's the fear and doubt
keeping me still and stuck, NOT life itself.

Working with a group of career shifters recently, I noticed a repeating story. One of being overwhelmed – by uncertainty, by the unknown, by the demands of 'everything else' – all wrapped up in one statement.

'I haven't got time.'

I haven't got time to figure out where to start. I haven't got enough time to do everything, so maybe it's best not to start right now. I haven't got time left after everything else is done (which of course it never is).

I haven't got time to sit with this uncertainty, this uncomfortable feeling – when the call of the dishes, the laundry and the inbox suddenly become increasingly insistent.

It's like the thinking itself uses up all of the available headspace, energy and oxygen – that there is nothing left for any of the doing.

Because it's not just the logical thinking – what to do; how to do it. It's the emotional thinking. What if I'm not good enough? What if this isn't me? What if it is? What's the right thing to do here? (And who am I if I get it wrong?)

The baggage we hold around not being enough (fast enough, impressive enough, fill-in-the-blank enough) makes us dismiss the whisper of wind that we do have. It sucks up the oxygen and keeps us stuck, weighing us down.

The worry that there isn't enough time, *that worry itself*, consumes all the time, headspace and emotional energy, and there's nothing left to take action or make progress with.

The more we wind ourselves up about it, the more we use up the wind, and the more stuck we become, under an ever-growing pile of 'should's', shame and self-doubt.

Surviving limbo

I'm told that one thing that helped those ancient mariners survive limbo was cleaning.

The weather was outside their control. They couldn't create wind. So they cleaned the decks and maintained the rigging. They stayed sane by doing what they could do, keeping the ship and themselves seaworthy, ready for when it was time to sail again.

In her book *Women Who Run With The Wolves*, psychoanalyst and post-trauma specialist Clarissa Pinkola Estés suggests that in some fairy tales, tasks like washing laundry and sweeping floors represent renewal, revival and caring for orderliness.

I must confess I railed when I read this – that somehow cleaning is good for a woman's soul. Yet I do find, to the dismay of my 21st-century feminist self, that when I'm riled up or restless, there is something satisfying and restorative about (a very short burst of) cleaning, sweeping up dust, clearing the cobwebs, folding clothes, resetting and restoring order to my space.

I find it endearing that some men do this too, according to the comedian Russell Kane, on the night after witnessing the birth of their baby, when they return home to spend that final night alone. What do they do? Among other things, they tidy up![24]

---

[24] Russell Kane, 'Kaneing: The night after the baby is born', 21 January 2018. Available from www.youtube.com/watch?v=TJyOoHiCZuw [accessed 17 November 2020].

Tending and trusting.

Maybe that's what we need when we find ourselves in limbo.

Tending to ourselves, our tools, our spaces. Keeping us fresh and ready for when the wind picks up again.

Holding space. Not trying to rush it or squeeze it.

Holding the space, feeling its weight. Trusting that this is the work right now. And that something important happens here.

Hold the space, feel its weight.

Trust that this is the work right now.

And that something important happens here.

The art of letting your work breathe

There are the dream moments, when inspiration grabs you, and ideas bubble over, and Work Just Flows.

In between those fleeting moments of brilliance are many more hours of awkward, agonizing, obscure, ambiguous, spluttering, stalling, wrangling Work.

Productivity is knowing when to work, and when to let the work breathe.

When we hold on too hard, we squeeze the life out of it – or out of us.

But when we don't hold on at all, the air dissipates, the ideas float into the ether. As Liz Gilbert puts it in her book *Big Magic*, the muse finds another artist who is willing to put in the work.

Our routines, structures and schedules are like the canvas of a hot-air balloon – a way of catching those fleeting thoughts as they rise, harnessing the raw ideas, bundling them together until eventually there's enough hot air to rise, momentum takes hold and we get lift off.

Breathing is an act of trust.
Inhale. Exhale. Expand. Contract. Refill. Release.

It's sitting with something patiently until it clicks.

It's walking away to let it skulk in your subconscious, until it's ready to surface.

And yes, it's starting your work early enough that you have time to do that.

Productivity is knowing when to work, and when to let the work breathe. Breathing is an act of trust.

Deep work

There's good work. And there's what is *seen* as good work. Those two things are not always the same.

So often, what is seen takes priority over what we know is good work.

Thinking. Absorbing. Learning. Building. Repairing. Brewing. Refuelling. Healing.

These are all things that can look outwardly unproductive, and yet are absolutely vital to doing good work.

When you go underground to dig deep.
And you worry that you'll be forgotten, overlooked.
That people will move on and all you have worked so hard to build
Your reputation, your platform, your following, your favour
May fall to ruin –
and it will all be your fault...

Know this.

You are seen.
You are showing up.
This matters.

The world will still be there.
And if people have moved on, so have you.

The deep undercover work you do is transformative.
It cannot be done in the spotlight.

Don't worry about where the world will be when you emerge.
Know where you will be.
Ready to take your place, to make waves.
To show up in all of your glory.
In the world as you find it.

A whirlpool of our own making

Sometimes being stuck doesn't look like stuck.
It doesn't look like you're stuck in one place. It looks like you're all over the place.

It looks a lot like busy.
Problems to fix. Emails to respond to. Thoughts to dissect. Arguments to have.

Where we get caught up in our own head – overthinking, ruminating, getting cross. Where we spend half a day composing a reply to that message that's triggered our email rage. Or wade in on someone else's project or problem, in order to avoid facing our own.

This kind of being stuck is deceptive. Because we don't notice it straight away.

It looks a lot like taking action, taking control.
Doing something about it.

We think we're fixing the problem when really we're just perpetuating the problem.

Caught up in a spell of activity and movement, we think we're doing something about it, but in reality we're whipping up a storm of things to do, to avoid doing the very thing we need to do.

A frenetic movement that keeps you stuck. Going nowhere fast. A whirlpool of our own making.

Needless struggle

S*ide note*: The journey involves struggle, but not all struggle is necessary.

Let's get comfortable with (but not reliant on) the discomfort.

While researching this book, I spoke to Angela Armstrong, author of *The Resilience Club*,[25] who spoke of her work in developing high-performing leaders, and her own experience in corporate life:

> Some of us get so used to the pattern of struggle, we get stuck in 'life is hard' and we forget to look for the easy solution.

If you've been used to fighting for everything you've achieved, it's easy to get caught up in expecting everything to be a fight.

Imagine being asked to sweep up Maltesers for example.

That's exactly what happened to Allan Leighton, chairman of The Co-operative Group and former CEO of Asda, in his early graduate trainee days at Mars.

Here's the story, as told by his publisher Nigel Wilcockson, publishing director at Random House Business Books:

> He had a humiliating first day where he was taken down the factory floor, handed a broom and they said to him, right, you sweep up any Maltesers that come off

---

[25] Angela Armstrong, *The Resilience Club: Daily Success Habits of Long-term High Performers*, 2019.

the conveyor belt... what followed was the three most embarrassing hours of his life as he chased these flipping Maltesers around the factory floor. And eventually one of the old lags came up to him, presumably with kind of a raised eyebrow and said, 'This is what you do.' And he simply put his foot down on the Malteser and he said, 'You squash them first, then you sweep them up.'[26]

Sometimes the struggle isn't in the hustle, bracing ourselves to stay the course and weather the storm. Sometimes it's asking ourselves, 'How can I let this be easy?'

'It has to be hard' can be just as limiting as 'it shouldn't be this hard'.

[26] *The Extraordinary Business Book Club* podcast, Episode 88 – 'The art of the business book with Nigel Wilcockson'. Available from http://extraordinarybusinessbooks.com/episode-88-the-art-of-the-business-book-with-nigel-wilcockson/?fbclid=IwAR3ffX3eAus7Z_RRZKxHNmhk60FDEteWhfKbCmoEHJd7KxiLD3ZcJYfwUNM [accessed 17 November 2020].

When we've got it wrong

Shit, I got it wrong

Such a hard thing to say in your head, let alone out loud. But it's one that keeps coming back round.

In how much unknowing is involved in navigating new territory.
In how much unlearning is involved in challenging structural racism.

And for me in parenting a teenager.

For much of the UK nationwide lockdown in the spring of 2020, my summary of how my kids were getting on had largely been 'Yeah they're fine, ploughing through their work. She's getting a bit bored; he's embracing the teenage life.'

Ten weeks in, messages started emerging from my son's school that suggested otherwise.

> 'We haven't heard from you since school closed. How
> are you getting on with the work?'

That moment when it hits you. When you thought everything was fine. And suddenly it's glaringly obvious that it's not.

Denial: *That can't be right. Must be a tech problem.*

Anger and blame: *Why didn't he say anything? Why didn't the school flag something earlier? Why didn't I spot this earlier? Why wasn't I more involved?*

Shame and guilt: *How stupid of me to think I could just leave him to it. I teach this stuff! How could I let it get this bad? I should have known better.*

Grief: *My poor boy. How much he's been struggling alone. How confused, disoriented, demoralized and overwhelmed he must have felt.*

Panic: *What else is wrong? How bad is this?*

Parenting is one of those areas where the pressure to get it right is so high.

Because the stakes are high. For families, it's our most important work.

And yet in many ways, there is no right. There is no perfection. No road map. No target. No definitive 'nailed it'.

So of course we'll get it wrong. How ridiculous to think we wouldn't?

Why is it so hard then to come to terms with when we do?

In parenting, we tell ourselves it's our job to hold it all together. To make the right call. There's no room for failure.

And we raise the stakes even higher when our identity is wrapped up in it.

Getting it wrong = being wrong = bad parent.

That's why it hits us so hard.

When our identity is at stake, it's scary what we will do to protect it.

How strong the urge was to defend my position, blame the school, blame my son, blame my husband, blame the technology (*which I'm still not convinced was entirely innocent*).

Or to swing to the other extreme. Tell myself how ridiculous it was to think a 14-year-old teenage boy could be trusted with so much freedom. To impose military law, micromanage every minute of his day, interrogate his every move – and consider it necessary because the opposite didn't work.

Or to crumble, abandon my values, my beliefs and my judgement, distrust myself entirely. Because clearly I don't know any better.

What made it worse was that I'd almost bragged about how I was refusing to call it home-schooling. That my children's work was theirs, not mine. And you weren't going to catch me panicking that I couldn't remember Pythagoras' theory.[27]

Nothing stings quite like the pain of a mother who feels like she's just been proven wrong.

---

[27] Although that didn't stop me from getting caught up one Friday afternoon trying to solve Question 9 of my 11 year old's Maths Challenge which clearly involved triangles.

Being wrong

So many of us struggle with getting it wrong because we see it as being wrong.

Our words stray from 'I got it wrong' to 'I am wrong'.

'I have' and 'I do' speak to our actions, our thoughts, our behaviours, which are changeable.

'I am' speaks to our identity, which feels permanent.

Perhaps that's why many people balk at being called a racist.

I've seen a government minister doggedly argue that there is no way a government whose party leader commissioned a report into institutional racism within its own ranks could possibly be racist – because they commissioned the report – despite the findings of the report itself.

I've seen caring, community-minded, Christian friends defend their use of 'All Lives Matter' as a loving and inclusive phrase because of what they mean by it, and argue that it's only problematic if you choose to see it that way.

I've had someone defend a racial microaggression to me, by insisting that it was I who took it personally and out of context, and refused to acknowledge harm done because he had not intended harm.

What I hear from all of these people is a refusal to entertain the possibility that they did (or are doing) something wrong – because they see themselves as being good people.

They feel the pain of cognitive dissonance – a term that's used to describe the mental discomfort we feel when our attitudes conflict with our behaviours – or in this case, when our identity conflicts with our actions.

They confuse the issue with their identity. And their brain goes into overdrive to defend their identity.

What's tragic is that whenever we dare to face the dissonance, it's not our identity that shatters, it's our actions that can change – to align more truly with our identity.

A responsible institution faces up to its flaws and does the work of dismantling structural inequality. A caring person changes their words to enact compassion rather than harm. A good friend apologizes for causing hurt, especially when it's unintended.

A good parent – I'm told by a friend with older kids – gets it right and wrong, which, of course, reminds me of my own mantra: to be a good enough mum most of the time, with intermittent lapses into brilliance and hopelessness.

The same goes for a good leader.

You are not the issue. You have an issue.
There isn't something wrong with you. You got something wrong.
You are not a failure. You failed at something.
Maybe you're not a racist, maybe some racism got inside you.

Let's not confuse the issue with our identity.

As we grow. As we navigate uncharted territory. As we unlearn old patterns. As we rewrite history. As we turn ourselves inside out. Let's commit to getting it right and wrong. Let's not be so afraid of getting it wrong that we do nothing, or dig our heels in. Let's not be so devastated by getting it wrong that we make it all about us.

Fear of getting it wrong leads to two extremes – silence or bigotry. Either I'm so afraid of doing wrong that I do nothing. Or I'm so afraid of being wrong that I erase the possibility of being wrong. I shut down anyone who says otherwise.

Both extremes are my ego talking.

Which is when I need to say to myself – with compassion, conviction and good humour –

Get over yourself, honey.

Beyond right and wrong

Maybe it's even worth rethinking our use of the words *right* and *wrong*.

Right and wrong are such fundamental ways we view the world. Good. Bad. Right. Wrong. Reward. Punishment. Carrot. Stick.

When my daughter was younger, one of the first questions she'd ask while watching a film was, 'Who's good? Who's bad?'

But right and wrong has its limits.

In organizations, too often we see deviation as wrong rather than the beginnings of an innovation.

In parenting, we send ourselves into spirals trying to get it right.

In society, the refusal to acknowledge wrong is precisely what creates bigotry.

In procrastination, the fear of being wrong is one of the biggest reasons we fail to put things right.

Because we just don't want to go there.

I don't want to get it wrong.
I need to prove why this is right.

Whether in an academic piece of work, a commercial decision, or moral judgement, we are so conditioned to look for right and wrong.

No one chooses to be wrong. We all think we are right.

But right and wrong is so one-dimensional. It doesn't give us language to describe new and different.

And in a moral argument, our desperation to cling to right and wrong so often means we don't listen. Right and wrong squeezes out understanding, empathy, consideration, recalibration, imagination.

So long as we're looking for right and wrong, we're not looking for new. We're not looking for different. We're looking for what fits with our picture of right. And discarding what doesn't.

So long as we're invested in being right, we will not truly listen. We seek to be accepted, we welcome those who agree with us and dismiss the voices that jar.

So long as we have to be right, we'll deflect with blame or drown in shame.

If we are never willing to be wrong, then we will almost definitely get it wrong.

When we put aside our need to be right, just for a moment, that's when we open ourselves up – to curiosity, to understanding, to empathy, to discovering.

To imagining and reimagining.

The world is a much richer place when we stop holding onto our need to be right.

Braver conversations

Beyond who's right, and who's wrong.
Beyond what's right and what's wrong.

Conversations that create, that collaborate, that build trust and understanding, that reimagine a new future.

What are we moving towards? What are we choosing?

These conversations require us to move beyond right and wrong.

Here are some great conversation builders that business psychologist Helen Frewin teaches in her work on honest conversations and feedback:

'Tell me more.'
'Help me understand.'

These are my go-tos for keeping a conversation open when someone's just said something that makes me want to shut down. Something that elicits a strong reaction – opposition, defensiveness, hurt, offence or WTF?!

I don't always remember to use it, but when I do, I never regret it. Sometimes it shows me the inaccuracy of the conclusion I was leaning towards. Sometimes it helps the other person clarify what they actually meant. Sometimes it turns out we are coming from different perspectives, but helps us to find common ground, or at least honour where the other person is coming from. Always, it helps us to feel heard.

'What's the most important thing about this for you?'

I learned this one recently in a marriage course. After nearly 18 years of marriage, we were both surprised at how this shifted the conversation.

We were talking about holidays. He was fed up with not being able to just make a decision and book it. Last time he came up with an idea, I wasn't keen on the flight times, and by the time we'd explored it further, the deal was no longer available and prices had gone up. He felt like his hands were tied. I felt like my voice was being dismissed. It looked a lot like a battle for control.

'What's the most important thing about this for you?' we asked each other.

Turns out what's important to him is a sense of adventure, space for spontaneity and value for money. What's important to me is rest – arriving ready to enjoy some rest and relaxation, rather than ready to collapse (and likely brewing a cold with our immune systems knocked). These no longer looked like opposing views. They were pieces of a puzzle that could fit together. Pieces we could work with.

Braver conversations are ones where we stay open rather than shut down. Open to understanding, to identifying, to seeing each other as fellow human beings rather than as the enemy or the opposition.

Othering allows us to justify our position. Of being right. The more we keep someone at a distance, the easier it is to rationalize our own thinking. And the easier it is for them to do the same.

The closer we get to understanding someone, the more we start to identify with them. It can cost us our certainty, our clear-cut, one-dimensional righteousness, but it gives us something far more powerful.

One person who understood this well was Nelson Mandela.

I was fascinated to read in Rutger Bregman's book *Humankind* about a conversation he had with his fiercest rival, Constand Viljoen, a military hero who was mobilizing for war.

> 'He asked me if I took tea,' Constand remembered years after the event. 'I said yes, and he poured me tea. Then he asked me if I took milk. I said yes, and he poured me milk. Then he asked me if I took sugar with my tea. I said I did and he poured the sugar. All I had to do was stir it!'

> As they talk, it's obvious that Mandela has made an effort to understand the history and culture of the Afrikaners, Constand is impressed when Mandela draws parallels between the Viljoen family's struggle for freedom from the British a hundred years ago and his own fight against apartheid. Most important, historians later note, is that Mandela talks to the military man in his own language. 'General' he says in Afrikaans, 'there can be no winners if we go to war.'

> Constand nods, 'There can be no winners.'

> That first meeting opens four months of secret talks between Viljoen and Mandela... In the end, the former

general was convinced to lay down his weapons and join the elections with his party.[28]

Mandela's understanding wasn't a mere tactic employed to manipulate his opponent. His understanding ran deep. As Bregman notes, when he was imprisoned:

> Mandela tried to make his fellow inmates see that their guards were people, too, only that they'd been poisoned by the system. Years later, that's how Mandela would look at Constand Viljoen: as an honest, loyal and brave man who'd spent his life fighting for a regime he believed in.[29]

---

[28] Rutger Bregman, *Humankind: A Hopeful History*, 2019, p. 357.

[29] Bregman, *Humankind*, p. 360.

The world is a much richer place when we stop holding onto our need to be right.

When we're spent

The morning after

The thing they often don't show in epic movies and tales of glory is the morning after. When the adrenaline and glory subsides, and is replaced with the aches, pains and fatigue.

The triumphant warrior who's now awkwardly creaking trying to avoid the sore spots of armour chafing and delayed-onset muscle soreness.

The marathon runner who's now hobbling slowly with a swollen ankle, while toddlers and pushchairs race past.

The times when you ache and creak, feeling flat and drained. When the adrenaline has left your system and you just need a lie down – or a good cry.

After the glory and the glamour of battle comes the morning after. The hangover that takes us by surprise.

My client Sarah was feeling flat. She couldn't really put her finger on why.

After all, this week was relatively quiet compared to the emotional rollercoaster of last week. But when we started talking about everything that had happened, we realized she had lived through a pretty traumatic time.

Post-traumatic hangover.

The hard work is done. The danger has passed. The victory is won.

That's when the rest of our body and brain functions kick back in. That's when we allow ourselves to feel and come to terms with the full force of what we've been through. That's when the adrenaline wears off and the pain sets in.

Interestingly, one of the functions of adrenaline is to decrease our ability to feel pain. Because pain's primary function is to tell us to stop. And when we're in fight or flight, the thing we must not do is stop.

It's only when we get to safety that we can stop. And that's when it all catches up with us.

That's when we experience the Let-Down Effect, 'a pattern in which people come down with an illness or develop flare-ups of a chronic condition not during a concentrated period of stress but after it dissipates' – which explains why so many people get ill when they take a holiday.[30]

So maybe if you're feeling shitty, your feelings aren't telling you the truth of what you're experiencing right now. They're telling you what you've been through.

There's nothing to fix in the here and now. It's what you've been through that needs acknowledging.

You're feeling shit not because you're going through shit, but because you've come through.

I've discovered that struggle has its own hangover too.

Once, over the course of ten days, I had delivered eight sessions and slept in ten different beds. Add in an incident of house gazumping and an emergency uniform shop, it was no

---

[30] Stacey Colino, 'The Let-Down Effect: Why you might feel bad after the pressure is off', *U.S. News*, 6 January 2016. Available from https://health.usnews.com/health-news/health-wellness/articles/2016-01-06/the-let-down-effect-why-you-might-feel-bad-after-the-pressure-is-off [accessed 17 November 2020].

wonder I got to the end and felt knackered. But what I wasn't prepared for was how long that exhaustion persisted.

It makes sense that if we pull out all the stops and go full on, that at some point we'll need to rest and recover. But we often don't see that coming. We think the hard work is done already, and now comes the easy bit.

My friend Josie finds that she gets the morning after feeling after really good days too. She has an autonomic nerve disorder which means that while parts of her body don't talk to each other properly, she also feels things far more keenly. To borrow a term from Glennon Doyle, she's our canary in the mineshaft. In many ways, what she notices acutely is what's going on for us under the surface. If Josie has an intensely good day – excitement, big news, a happy surprise – she'll need a very long lie down the next day.

Perhaps not unlike the child who bursts into tears on her birthday, or when she finally gets that puppy.

This is part of the struggle too. The wobble that comes after the intensity. It helps to know it's normal, and instead of beating ourselves up with how we think we 'should' feel, to give ourselves space to recover and let the rest of us catch up with what just happened.

Catch up

I once read somewhere that our brain's emotional processing is much slower than our mental processing. Try this as an experiment:

> Think of a fish. Now an elephant. Now a cup of tea. Now a clock tower. Now a cucumber.

> Now, imagine feeling excitement. Now embarrassment. Now grief. Now gratitude.

Takes longer to switch doesn't it?

In my work, I often use the term cognitive load to describe the amount of mental processing involved in daily life and work. That what's overwhelming isn't just the number of things to do, but the number of decisions we need to make about those things – and the amount of information processing that entails.

But what about the emotional load? The disappointment when someone lets us down; the guilt and shame when we fall short; the confusion or frustration when we don't understand someone's behaviour; the grief when a relationship, or a season, comes to an end.

The pace so many of us operate at these days barely gives room for breath, let alone the full processing of these emotions. We rush on, fixating on what we need to do rather than face up to how we feel.

I wonder if that's one of the reasons why so few people truly rest. Because when we do, that's when these things catch up with us. The tsunami of emotions we're constantly trying to outrun.

When we quit pacing, thinking, fixing and fixating – on deals and decisions, strategies and systems, people and problems – we come face to face with our feelings, and what that tells us about ourselves.

Not always pretty

Because self-care isn't all spa days and smoothies.

And rest is not always pretty.

Rest is where we might turn round to the person we're with – or the person we've become – and think, *I'm not sure I like you any more.*

Rest is where we face up to the cognitive dissonance. All the times where we've fallen short of who we want to be. The times we've chosen 'right' over relationship, or being clever over being compassionate. The times when we've snapped or yelled, that had everything to do with us and nothing to do with them. The times when, instead of working on our hurt, we've worked it out on someone else. The times when we've been the lousy friend, colleague, boss or partner.

Rest is an act of trust. Not a serene, smiling trust. But a wincing, white-knuckled, oh-heck-here-we-go kind of trust.

Rest is terrifying.

Why it's terrifying to rest

Ever catch yourself thinking, *I'm not sure I want to do this any more?*

When everything feels uphill, or humdrum. When the work has lost its colour, or you've lost your mojo. And you find yourself thinking, *what the heck am I doing here?*

When it happens in small doses, we call it a blip. When it hits hard and doesn't shift, we call it burnout. I've known people get floored by this.

But what if the answer isn't to avoid it, but to embrace it regularly?

You see, when things get hard, our instinct is to hold on tighter – make it work, make the ideas come, push through the fog.

But what if the reverse is actually what we need?

Let go. Drop it. Walk away.

That's exactly what Rob Bell does, as he describes in his podcast 'What Happens Every Six Months'.

> I would get so uninterested in what I do. Zero mojo. Zero energy. All of my ideas would just shrivel up... I don't really feel like talking, I don't have anything to say, maybe it's all over?

Instead of ignoring that feeling or trying to push it away, Rob decided to follow it to see where it would lead.[31]

He let himself drift. To stop creating. Stop producing. And walk away from it all.

Anybody else find this terrifying? Or is it just me?

I think this is why we find it so hard to rest, to switch off completely: we're terrified that if we let go, we'll lose it all – or lose ourselves.

What if it all falls apart? Or worse, doesn't fall apart and it becomes blindingly obvious that I'm not needed at all?!

What if I lose it all because I took my eye off the ball? The opportunities, the credibility, the community, the momentum – everything I've worked so hard to build?

What if I don't want to come back at all? What if I lose my edge, my mojo, my spark? What if I drift away forever?

Except we don't.

We discover perspective.

Rob would look at his work and go, 'Wait, that's what I do? That is a strange way to work!'

Sometimes we can take ourselves and our work far too seriously. To be able to step back, to look at our work with marvel, wonder or just plain 'what the heck?!' gives us a chance to reset and see things from a new perspective.

We make peace with what we can't control. According to Rob:

---

[31] Rob Bell, 'What Happens Every 6 Months' podcast, Episode 205, 19 August 2018. Available from https://robbell.podbean.com/e/what-happens-every-6-months [accessed 17 November 2020].

> When you take your hand off the wheel, you are forced
> to come to terms with all the ways you've been trying
> to control things that aren't allowing you to control
> them.

I see this happen sometimes with a workshop delegate who is so stressed by someone else's behaviour that it dominates their attention. To the point where they refuse to use the workshop to focus on their own workload, habits and decisions – things that would actually help and that they do have control over – because they're holding so tightly onto the thing that somebody else has or hasn't done.

Rob calls this grasping energy. A toxic, frustrating loop that builds up when we keep trying to control, manipulate or force things into place and it's just not working.

And it's not always because we explicitly want to control others. It can happen when we care too much, and grasp too tightly. The problem is, we can't care all the time. 'The heart can only care so much, then it needs a break. It needs a release valve.'[32]

We find our way back.

After a while, there would come a day when he'd stumble on an idea and think, 'oh that's interesting!' which would remind him of something, and connect with something else. One idea leads to another. As Rob says, 'All of a sudden, I'd find myself making things and getting back into the groove.'

We don't drift forever. We find our way back, with more energy and more vitality.

---

[32] Bell, 'What Happens Every 6 Months' podcast.

Rest has a funny way of stripping off the ego, and reinvigorating the soul. When your work starts to lose its edge or its colour, maybe the answer is to walk away. Trust that it's ok to be lost for a while, and know that you won't be lost forever.

Perhaps because wherever you walk to – there you are.

What changes is the baggage you strip off along the way. The control, the ego, the proving. The obligations and expectations of what success should look like. The stuff that doesn't belong to you. The stuff you've been clinging on too tightly to.

You find yourself again.

Your mojo. Your spark. Your edge. Your imagination. Your compassion.

And let's face it, when we hold on too tightly for too long, we lose the things we're desperately trying to hold onto anyway. We have less and less imagination. Less and less compassion. Less and less energy.

Sometimes you have to walk away to find out just which bits you'd really miss.

Sometimes you have to release control to realize how much power you really have.

Sometimes you have to walk away to find out just which bits you'd really miss.

Sometimes you have to release control to realize how much power you really have.

Seasons and cycles

Technology can be 24/7. Human beings can't.

For anything that has life, a flat line is generally not a good sign.

There was a time when we were shaped by natural rhythms in life: the setting of the sun marked the end of a productive day; winter in agricultural life was generally a fallow season. We had natural beginnings, endings and pauses to guide our rhythms of work.

In enabling us to work anytime, technology has also disabled us by taking away our natural pauses and rhythms of recovery and reflection. Technology may have removed the natural limitations of daylight and communication delays but our human need for rhythm remains.

Perhaps the limitations we thought were holding us back were really holding us together.

When we work without breaks, our judgement deteriorates with decision fatigue. When we extend the day and sacrifice our sleep, our cognitive impairment can be on par with being drunk.

Throughout the working day, our energy and attention levels fluctuate, and yet our expectation is that our output will be constant throughout. Day by day, month by month, year by year, our tendency is to rush from one thing to another, chasing the work that never ends, with little pause, reflection or recalibration.

It's time to bring back a cyclical nature to our rhythm. To intentionally create pauses and endings.

Breaks. Sabbaticals. Seasons.

My colleague, Graham Allcott, has zoned his day into what he calls the 3Cs. Create. Collaborate. Chill. Generally, mornings are his Create time, where he does his best thinking uninterrupted. Afternoons are then dedicated to meetings and conversations of collaboration, primarily supporting others. Evenings are his Chill time, a time to down tools and recharge.

A few years ago, coming towards the end of a particularly intensive year of travel, workshop delivery and book promotion, I picked up the musician Amanda Palmer's book, *The Art of Asking*, in which she describes three aspects of the creative cycle: Collecting, Connecting and Sharing. Collecting is where you gather your materials, your supplies, your ideas. Connecting is where you join the dots – metaphorically or literally – to create something new. Sharing is where you take it out into the world.

I'm a natural sharer, so much of my work – speaking, coaching, training – is well suited to that. Writing is my primary connector. Yes, there's a sharing element to that too when you hit publish, but the act of writing is how my ideas come together. What I realized at that point in my life was that I was all shared out. As much as I loved it, I had nothing more to give, nothing new to give – and what I needed to pay attention to was collecting. Reading, listening to other people speak, learning, gathering different materials to work with.

Companies go through seasons of start-up, scale up, expansion and consolidation. Agriculture has its seasons of ploughing, sowing, tending, reaping and resting. We have our personal seasons too.

In a season of high change or new starts, you might need extra space to navigate the thousand tiny decisions involved. Or if you're currently in a season of establishing, settling in and growing roots, it's perfectly ok not to be launching something 'new'.

We were never designed to do everything at once. So let's stop confusing our ploughing with our reaping. Or a fallow season with a failed harvest.

Efficiency or deficiency?

While we're on the subject of farming, let's talk about wheat – or bread specifically.

My friend Bex is obsessed with bread. She runs Ear To Ground Bakehouse, a micro-bakery, from her home in Leicester. If you live locally, I'd highly recommend you check out her Bread Drop service.

Last time I visited her, she educated me on the industrialization of bread making. I always thought this just meant that bread was made in factories instead of by hand. Turns out there's a whole lot more to it than that.

Firstly, in agriculture, we swapped traditional farming methods and crops for intensive mass farming. Land was cleared of trees, hedgerows and bushes to allow more space for intensive wheat farming. Botanists narrowed the genetic diversity of wheat, favouring a higher yield monoculture, which relied heavily on fertilizers and pesticides.

This lack of diversity, plus the addition of chemicals, in turn compromised the nutritional value of the soil. What's more, intensively grown modern wheat is unable to grow deep roots, so is unable to access the nutrient-richest part of the soil.

The drive towards monoculture is so pervasive that, more recently, a scientist who succeeded in breeding a more genetically diverse, nutrient-rich and resilient wheat crop found that it could not be legally registered or traded in Europe, because the commercial legislature is such that seeds and plant varieties must be identified singularly and conform to certain criteria for uniformity and stability.[33]

Next, in processing flour, millers exchanged stoneground mills for steel rollers, which are very efficient at separating the component parts of the grain, but also strip out most of the micronutrients concentrated in the outer layers of the germ, leaving the endosperm, 'a pure starch so nutritionally void that by UK law vitamins must be added back into white flour'.[34] The rollers also get hot in the process, which significantly reduces the wild yeast or lactic acid bacteria that might be present in the flour.

Finally, bakers who used quality ingredients and slow fermentation methods (which allow good bacteria cultures to develop) were replaced by large-scale industrial factories where bread is made using fast-acting industrialized yeast which enables bread to be produced at a rapid rate. At this rate, bread isn't able to develop the wealth of lactic acid bacteria found in real bread, making it less nutritious and nourishing, and also harder on people with digestive problems. It's also here where a bunch of additives are put in in order to extend the shelf life of the bread.

At every stage of the process – from crop selection, to agricultural methods, manufacturing and baking – the drive for efficiency has stripped bread of its nutritional value and the end result is deficiency.

---

[33] Wendell Steavenson, 'Flour power: Meet the bread heads baking a better loaf', *The Guardian*, 10 October 2019. Available from www.theguardian.com/food/2019/oct/10/flour-power-meet-the-bread-heads-baking-a-better-loaf [accessed 17 November 2020].

[34] Steavenson, 'Flour power', *The Guardian*, 10 October 2019.

The same thing happens with our obsession with efficiency at work.

In focusing solely on doing more for less and getting stuff done faster:

We stop thinking. We get so focused on the doing, we don't give ourselves time to think.

We stop discerning. As Peter Drucker put it, 'There is surely nothing quite so useless as doing with great efficiency what should not be done at all.'[35] I wonder, how much work do we create for ourselves and each other, because we were so focused on getting stuff done that we didn't stop to ask if it should be done at all?

We stop listening. We tell, we shout, we send another email and schedule yet another meeting. We create noise, trying to get our message through – and when something does reach our ears, we jump straight into either defensive or problem-solving mode, forgetting to just listen first.

We stop stopping. We value motion over progress. We fill in all the blank spaces. Working through lunch. Tweeting on the loo. Emailing on our commute. Frenetic pace becomes the norm and stopping becomes unusual, uncomfortable, feared or even derided.

We stop caring. Either because we're burnt out – or in some cases, we've streamlined the work so much that all we do is follow a series of tick boxes and scripts. Work becomes completely devoid of meaning and dangerously lacking in care, compassion or humanity.

---

[35] Peter Drucker, 'Managing for business effectiveness', *Harvard Business Review*, May 1963. Available from https://hbr.org/1963/05/managing-for-business-effectiveness [accessed 17 November 2020].

We stop trusting. In optimizing performance, we add in measures that take away autonomy and ownership, replacing them with bureaucracy, data and targets that result in people spending more time servicing the system than serving the clients, patients or community.

We stop questioning. When everyone's frantically busy meeting deadlines, questions are disruptive and frowned upon. 'Because I said so' and 'just get on with it' becomes the default answer – whether spoken or not. What's more, we surround ourselves with people who are just like us – like-minded people are less likely to debate, differ or disagree, so less time is 'wasted'. Our echo chambers get louder and our blind spots get larger when we sacrifice diversity for the sake of uniformity.

We stop learning. When there's no time to think, we stick with what we know – or asking who we know. Those with expertise get inundated with interruptions, and those without it never learn, because it's always quicker to ask than to risk the time it takes to actually learn it for yourself.

We stop innovating. Efficiency is about doing the familiar faster. Streamlining, smoothing, ordering. Innovation is about stepping into the unfamiliar. Taking risks. Breaking things. Disrupting the status quo. Getting things wrong. Going back. Going sideways. Going round in circles. Often the steps that lead to innovation look incredibly inefficient.

The crazy thing is that efficiency is what robots do really well. Us humans? It's the care, the compassion, the collaboration and the creativity that we have a unique handle on. The very things that get stripped out in our pursuit of efficiency, creating a deficiency in how we live and work.

The road we make by walking

Success is not a straight line

Heck, it's not even one line.

Success is a labyrinth. Detours, dead ends, doorways, discoveries. We find our way; we lose our way. Along the way, we discover guardians, teachers, tricksters, allies, mysterious keys and potent powers.

We're so used to seeing the filtered version, the edited highlights, that we forget – every adventure has its disappointments and failures, its betrayals and compromises.

On screen and on the page, we cry with our heroes when they are left battered by external forces. We scream 'no!' at them when they allow their inner demons to steal them away or shut them down, because we know they could do so much better.

But we don't vilify them, scoff at them, write them off as stupid, belittle or abandon them. We love them more for their flaws and failings.

No, that kind of punishment we reserve for ourselves.

The messy middle

If what you're working on looks like a mess at the moment, take comfort in knowing that's exactly what the middle looks like.

Rooms get messier before they get tidier.
Mess gives space for change.

We need space to unpick and unravel before we can recreate something new.

Sometimes struggle is simply giving ourselves the space to walk a longer, more complex journey, and resisting the temptation to tie it up in a nice neat, efficient bow.

I notice when I'm in struggle, the temptation to stray into black-and-white territory is high. My brain doesn't like open loops and unanswered questions. It lurches into action to make up an ending, to jump to a conclusion, to finish the sentence.

Conflict becomes reduced to good and evil. Blame and shame. Right and wrong. In an argument with my husband, either he's wrong and I'm right, or I'm right and he's wrong. Whereas the reality is so much more complex and confusing than that. Often, we're both wrong and we're both right. How flipping annoying is that?!

Maybe in our black-and-white view we're missing the bigger, far more colourful picture. Maybe we need to sit in the dark room of inconclusions and confusion for now – in order to let the rest of the picture develop.

As the saying goes, you can't spoil an ugly baby.

If something's too perfect, we won't want to mess with it. But if it's already a mess, we have full permission, invitation even, to play, dismantle, experiment and recreate.

I love how Tim Harford's book *Messy*[36] opens with the story of a 17-year-old German student, Vera Brandes, who had booked renowned improvisation jazz pianist Keith Jarrett to play at the Cologne Opera House.

When Jarrett turned up to practice, it turned out the piano that had been delivered was entirely inadequate: 'completely out of tune, the black notes in the middle didn't work, the pedals stuck. It was unplayable...'[37] Jarrett's instinct was to pull out and not play. And it was only out of pity for Brandes that he agreed to play.

What transpired was the performance of a lifetime. The recording, *The Köln Concert album*, became the best-selling solo jazz and solo piano album of all time.

The piano's many defects forced him to play in a completely different way, departing from what he knew into completely foreign territory, producing something unique. 'It wasn't the music that he ever imagined playing. But handed a mess, Keith Jarrett embraced it, and soared.'[38]

What mess do you get to play with today?

---

[36] Tim Harford, *Messy: How To be Creative and Resilient in a Tidy-Minded World*, 2016.

[37] Harford, *Messy*, p. 2.

[38] Harford, *Messy*, pp. 3–4.

What mess do you get to play with today?

A beautiful life

If your life is a mess right now, because you've been doing the deep work of unpicking. Because you've been brave and gone below deck. Because you're facing your demons, and taking the harder, truer path. Then, know this:

You have a beautiful life.

Not because you play it safe and get everything just right. But because you're willing to be brave, to show up, to get scared, to ride the rollercoaster.

There are times when you don't see the beauty, because the mess screams too loudly at you. But I promise you, the beauty is there, right there in the mess.

It is there because you are there.
Beautiful one.

Beauty is not always pretty.

Beauty is in the new mother, with her sweaty face, matted hair and mismatched shoes.
Beauty is in the wrinkles and scars that tell a lifetime of stories.
Beauty is in the ugly crying, snot, tears and all, of a secret shared, a loss mourned, a trauma released.

Beauty was in what Elaine Halligan called her lowest parenting moment, a time when, on a crowded train, her son Sam started kicking one of the other passengers, and she was powerless to stop him. 'What your boy needs is discipline – a darned good smack will sort him out,' said the passenger at full volume, increasingly (and understandably) upset. 'I felt hopeless, embarrassed, and completely out of control' recalls Elaine.

> I didn't know what to do and then out of nowhere... I heard myself making a speech: 'My child is autistic. I need your support, not judgement, as I am dealing with a disabled child... He is not being a problem, but having a problem. As you can see, I am not coping well, but the last thing in the world I am going to do is to smack my child for having a problem. Will you all please stop judging me and will someone help me to leave the train at the next station.'

> The silence was excruciating.

> Then another passenger spoke out. 'Yeah leave that poor lady alone – she's doing the best job she can.' And in an instant, the whole carriage descended into a heated argument about how to discipline a child, whether I was doing it right or wrong, how little we understand about autism, and whether or not smacking is an effective form of discipline. Sam sat wide-eyed and silent as he observed all the adults around him behave like they were having a playground slanging match.[39]

Elaine sees this as her lowest parenting moment. And while I absolutely feel the ache, I also see the beauty of a mother standing with and for her child, articulating and advocating for their needs rather than shrinking into apology to keep the peace. I see the wonder of a child who struggled to manage his emotions see a glimpse of the exact same thing play out in well-adjusted adults.

---

[39] Elaine Halligan, *My Child's Different: The Lessons Learned from One Family's Struggle to Unlock Their Son's Potential*, 2018, p. 76.

Beauty is in the lean on the shoulder, the catching of breath, the crumple of paper, the sweat of the brow, the dusty knees and grazed elbows, the outstretched hand, the soggy shoulder.

The cave you fear

The cave you fear to enter holds the treasure you seek.

Attributed to Joseph Campbell

Here's the truth. Avoiding something doesn't make it disappear.

Inaction doesn't freeze time. It freezes you.

Silence has its own voice.

There's a saying: if you want something badly enough, you'll make it happen. It's meant to be motivational, but often has the opposite effect. Because it shames us into believing that if we avoid something, it's because we don't want it enough.

But procrastination isn't always a sign that you don't want something. It can also be a sign that you really want something.

Nerves are a sign that we care.

Resistance is a sign that says: this is the work that really matters.

We've been reading the signs all wrong.

Fear reads: Danger, keep out.

Courage reads: This is sacred ground. Enter.

Fear reads: Danger, keep out.

Courage reads: This is sacred ground. Enter.

The truth about courage

Courage is not the absence of fear.
It's what we do in the face of it.

It's our relationship with fear.

One that says, 'Ok, I'll look. I'll go there' or 'Ok, I'll feel' instead of numbing and distracting.
One that says 'Ok, I'll rest. I'll let go. And trust what I come back to.'
One that says 'This may go wrong. In fact, it probably will. And I haven't got it all together. I'm probably not enough. I most definitely am not in control of it all. And... it's still worth doing.'

And in the words of Liz Gilbert's wonderful letter to fear:

> I recognize and respect that you are part of this family, and so I will never exclude you from our activities, but still – your suggestions will never be followed. You're allowed to have a seat, and you're allowed to have a voice, but you are not allowed to have a vote. You're not allowed to touch the road maps; you're not allowed to suggest detours; you're not allowed to fiddle with the temperature. Dude, you're not even allowed to touch the radio. But above all else, my dear old familiar friend, you are absolutely forbidden to drive.[40]

---

[40] Elizabeth Gilbert, *Big Magic: How to Live a Creative Life, and Let Go of Your Fear*, 2015.

The tunnel

We often talk about light at the end of the tunnel. The resolution, the prize, the relief, the happily ever after.

But I'm convinced that what we need, more than ever, is light in the middle of the tunnel.

Because there's work to be done in the tunnel. It's not just about racing through to the other side. And for that, we need light.

Light that shines on the work that needs to be done, and the work that's in progress.
Light that shines on the treasure in the dirt, and the beauty in imperfection, mystery and incompleteness.

Light that defines substance from shadow, and reveals contrast and paradox.
Light that revives our strength, conviction, compassion and sense of humour.

Light that reminds us to see each other.
Light that reminds us we're not alone.
Light that reveals we are powerful beyond measure.

Dead ends, new beginnings

When you hit a dead end – and you will – know that there's always a new beginning.

The end of the world as we know it is the beginning of everything else.

PART THREE

Stronger

Embrace the growth

What if we stopped believing struggle to be a sign of weakness or failure? We become stronger. We stretch. We grow. This is the stronger way to live and grow in struggle.

Struggle strengthens

Mountains

Now, every time I witness a strong person, I want
to know: What dark did you conquer in your story?
Mountains do not rise without earthquakes.

Katherine MacKenett[41]

---

[41] Katherine MacKenett, Instagram post, 22 August 2018. Available from www.
instagram.com/p/Bmw88IEBxN7 [accessed 17 November 2020].

We can do hard things

'**M**ummy I need you!'

That's the sum of all my babies' cries.

I'm hungry. I'm tired. I'm too hot. Too cold. I'm sad, I'm hurt, I'm bored. I need you to fix it for me.

Somewhere along the years, that changed.

The problem with being the fixer is you get good at it. And then one day you realize they no longer need you to be the fixer.

They need to know that they too can fix things. They need to learn how to fix things for themselves.

And when I continue to fix things for them, they can't learn that.

But when you're the pro fixer and they're the novice fixer, the temptation is still high:

'It's not that hard.'
'Let me show you...'
'Let me do that for you...'

And what they hear is:

'This shouldn't be hard. There's something wrong... maybe it's with me. Maybe I can't do it.'

So here's what I've learned to say instead:

'I know it's hard.'
'You're right, honey, that sucks.'
'I get it, I struggle too.'

What my kids need more from me now is not a fixer. They need my compassion, my empathy, my vulnerability, my humanity. They need to know that I struggle too. And that struggle doesn't mean it's all gone wrong, or that there's something wrong with them.

Struggle is normal.

Struggle is how we learn. How we develop. How we become capable. How we discover just how capable we can be.

In the words of Brené Brown, 'the most uncomfortable learning is often the most powerful'.[42]

And in the words of Glennon Doyle, 'We can do hard things.'

---

[42] Brené Brown, 'Your weekly dose of daring'. Newsletter, 4 June 2018.

Stretch and growth

There's not much stretch in the comfort zone, and unfortunately there's not much comfort in the stretch zone either.

Jenny Ainsworth

My friend Jenny is one of the strongest, brightest people I know. She is full of confidence, courage and energy. Her great big smile is matched only by the size of her heart. With her down-to-earth wit and wisdom, and her broad Yorkshire accent, she lights up the room in every way. One senior director of a global organization even described her as 'like having a shot of human caffeine'.

When you first meet Jenny, you think she's one of those people who's got it nailed. She's where she is because she's brave. Which is true. But she'll also tell you that stretching is not a one-time event, and having recently left a 25-year broken marriage, being brave means facing up to the reality of pain.

I have run, and run, and run. I am exhausted running. I could run rings around Mo Farah! Because of that fear, that it's going to hurt, it's going to be painful, it's going to be horrible, I don't want to go there. And the fact of the matter is, it is going to hurt and it is going to be painful. But the question I have is, are you free of pain now? And my answer was no, no I'm not.

The choice wasn't between pain and no pain. It was between a destructive pain that kept her in the dark, bound up, hemmed in, unable to move or see beyond the pain – and growth pain, something akin to labour pain: 'it still hurts and it's still horrible, but it's the right kind of pain. Healing pain.'

It is a pain that you can stand within and find strength, knowing that something good will come of it. It's still dark, but you can adjust your eyes to see in the dark, to see more than just the pain.

Stretch is how we grow. When we grow, we get growing pains. Sometimes we think the pain means we should stop and retreat. That we've hit our limit or gone too far.

And yes, as my yoga teacher tells me, we can overdo it, so it's good to listen to our bodies. But perhaps we could do with relearning the language of our bodies.

Perhaps the resistance is saying yes, right here. This is the area that needs a good stretch. Go easy, but keep going.

And the burn is telling us that our muscles are being made stronger – literally a process of micro-tears and rebuilding.

A while back, I was told a story about trees inside a sealed biome, which grew tall but weak. Without wind, I was told, they didn't grow strong roots. When I looked it up, it turns out it wasn't the roots that were missing; it was the presence of what's known as stress wood, or reaction bark, a type of wood that grows in reaction to strong winds, to make the tree stronger and more pliable to bending without breaking.[43]

Struggle is how we grow.

---

[43] Wikipedia, 'Biosphere 2'. Available from https://en.wikipedia.org/wiki/Biosphere_2 [accessed 17 November 2020].

And sometimes growth isn't necessarily outwards, but more of a returning to a shape and a size that's truer, after being contorted and conditioned for so long.

As Jenny said:

I felt like I've been living in a house where no doors or windows had been open for years, and all of a sudden I'd flung open the windows and I thought 'Ahh I can breathe!' I did not realize how much I was not breathing. Just shallow breaths to keep me going. And now I was gulping in air. That was quite profound.

Out of my depth

'I'm feeling out of my depth.'

'Good. Because that means you'll be brave.'

So often we believe that being out of our depth disqualifies us. That it means we're not cut out for it. Yet more often the opposite is true. Being out of our depth is exactly the conditions that call us to grow, to stretch, to rise, to be brave. To emerge anew.

That's when we need to hear 'good, that's exactly right for you' rather than 'you're not right for this'.

When you think, *I'm not sure I'm ready for this*.

You're so ready for this.

Resilience, not immunity

What makes you strong – and the perfect candidate – is not because you don't have all the other things going on, but that you continually keep rising and recovering from those things.

In other words, it's not that you don't fall down, it's that you keep getting up.

It is your resilience, not your immunity, that determines your strength.

I wrote these words in a comment on my friend Al's post. Al was preparing for a suitability assessment for a physical rehabilitation and pain management programme to help her manage the effects of EDS.

EDS – Ehlers-Danlos syndrome – is a term given to a group of connective tissue disorders that are generally characterized by hyper mobility, skin hyper-extensibility, tissue fragility and poor wound healing. Basically, the parts of our body that are supposed to move or stretch can stretch too much, damage easily and have a hard time healing.

For Al, this means, among other things, daily dislocations, constant pain, cardiac and respiratory issues, being wheel-chair-mobile, having a PEG feeding tube fitted (recently refitted to feed directly into the intestine after the first PEG became infected and unviable), and becoming very familiar with hospitals up and down the country.

The rehab programme was a challenging one with very specific admissions criteria. At an intake of only three new patients a week, it was in very high demand. The consultant who referred her warned that they would try to screen her out as a lost cause, because she also had Bilateral Ménière's[44] disease, PoTS[45] and depression.

Whenever we apply for something – a job, a course, a medical programme – we think it is our successes that qualify us. We look for obvious strengths, natural talent and straightforward fit, while seeing weakness, struggle and additional complications as potential sources of disqualification.

But does that really have to be the case?

It is your resilience, not your immunity, that determines your strength.

Al took this line to heart, and shared it in her assessment, along with a request not to attend a mass pity party, which they found very funny. The response was overwhelmingly positive. 'Wow, fantastic attitude,' they said, and she was in, there and then.

Even though, technically, she wasn't healthy enough for the usual admission criteria, she demonstrated she had the mental stamina and attitude to push through and deal with it, and indeed benefit even more from the programme than some healthier patients.

---

[44] Ménière's disease is a condition of the inner ear that causes sudden attacks of vertigo, tinnitus, pressure inside the ear and hearing and balance loss.

[45] Postural tachycardia syndrome (PoTS) is an abnormal increase in heart rate that occurs after sitting up or standing. Some typical symptoms include dizziness and fainting.

Her three weeks at the Royal National Orthopaedic Hospital were an incredible experience. In Al's words, 'intense, painful, stretching, educational and mind blowing'.

The rehab programme was designed to examine, understand and then challenge thresholds, both physically and mentally. It worked by establishing a baseline, understanding the swings around that baseline and then in tiny ways expanding or adapting an element slightly, working towards personally meaningful targets of function and quality of life. The process often felt like taking one step forward and two steps back.

> There were moments when I wasn't sure I could face the next movement, dislocation, breath or heartbeat. The love, kindness, support of staff and patients carried me through. We managed to fit in plenty of laughter, pranking, singing, pampering, thankfulness, sunbathing, even spending time at the radio station introducing tracks and hopefully helping others smile. New activities (creatively adapted as required) like balancing on gym balls, table tennis, badminton, curling, clay sculpting, and my old favourite, swimming. So many boundaries were expanded physically, emotionally and spiritually.

Indeed, Al found that the whole process to managing pain, gaining independence and a fresh perspective was never about finding a cure, numbing, restricting or closing down – all of which she had been doing before.

Instead, 'I have decided to embrace pain, accept it, learn to live with it and experiment.'

Her most recent experiment involves ordering a specialist recumbent trike that cost £5,000.

> My bank account certainly felt a flash of pain but my heart sang at the thought of not being trapped inside unable to wheel far with hands or join A&E [her husband and their son] in their cycling adventures.

She has no doubt there will be pain and frustration involved in learning to operate such a different piece of equipment, navigating other road users, maintaining it, as well as the ongoing insurance expense. But for now, knowing that she won't be the perfect speed cyclist, road user, mechanic or have pain-free or dislocation-free riding, means that she's actually more ready to embrace the very thoughts, emotions and sensations that she was trying to protect herself from before.

> That simple line of 'resilience not immunity makes me strong' started a process that's positively impacted in dimensions I had never expected.

I get knocked down

Do the best you can until you know better. Then when you know better, do better.

Maya Angelou

As a recovering perfectionist, it's safe to say I've struggled with failure. Somehow I always equate it to 'not enough'. Not having done enough, or being competent or confident or savvy enough.

I should have known better is the go-to for a perfectionist. I should have known better, then I would have done better. I seem to have Dr Angelou's advice back to front.

The problem with that is it's always looking backwards. We perfectionists get so caught up with getting knocked down, we forget that it's the getting back up that matters.

After all, isn't that how babies learn to walk? Perpetual falling, catching yourself, getting back up.

My husband has a completely different attitude to falling down. He treats it as a familiar companion. Growing up with dyslexia in one of the only local educational authorities at the time that didn't recognize it, there were many times where he failed – in assignments, spelling tests, being picked on to read aloud in class.

What he learned as a by-product was resilience and ingenuity. He discovered that if you taped five Bic pens together, they were perfectly spaced to write lines five times faster. He advocated to his headteacher that it would be pointless for him to continue with a modern language at GCSE since he couldn't even grasp English grammar let alone French – and took an extra Science instead.

On top of that, his home life was turbulent. 'My dad would always make promises, he loves to be the hero. Then once you're relying on him, he'd pull the rug from under your feet.'

My husband was no stranger to falling down. And because of that, he was no stranger to getting up either. He'd had plenty of practice.

Despite flunking his A-levels and living on the breadline for a while, he later decided to re-enrol at college and ended up on a foundation year course that led to a degree in Software Engineering, and in recent years has also completed his Masters in Mobile Device Application Development.

His story is by no means an isolated case.

Agatha Christie, Albert Einstein, Eleanor Roosevelt, Erin Brockovich, Leonardo da Vinci, Richard Branson, Steven Spielberg, Whoopi Goldberg, to name but a few, are all famous dyslexics who went on to achieve great things – and many of them attribute their familiarity with struggle and resilience as key factors to their success.

The thing about knowing failure is that you know what it feels like. You recognize it. The shock of it doesn't floor you, and the fear of it doesn't hold you back. You know where you are and you know what to do – get back up, find a way round, or a way through.

That's the thing that's often missing for kids who are so well provided for and sheltered from struggle, often by well-meaning parents who don't want their children to have to go through the same hardship that perhaps they did.

This is perfectly summarized in a scene from the screen adaptation of *Little Fires Everywhere*, which shows Lexie, the eldest daughter in a wealthy, privileged family, struggling with the topic of her Yale admissions essay – to write about a hardship that she has overcome.[46]

Her mother's response is telling of both privilege and perfectionism:

> Your father and I worked very hard your entire life to prevent you from having any hardship and now you have to go and try to drum one up… I feel like they're sort of saying if you're not raised by a crack-addicted mother who can barely make ends meet, what? Do you get punished for it? That's silly.

As an example of privilege, it landed with the intended dramatic effect: *'No, she didn't just say that?!'* but uncomfortably, the perfectionist in me did recognize something in it.

A case of mistaken identity.

Where we think the answer to having a good life is to do everything possible to stay standing, to avoid falling, rather than know that you have what it takes to get back up.

---

[46] *Little Fires Everywhere.* Drama miniseries, *Hulu*, 18 March to 22 April 2020.

Struggle is how we learn.
How we develop.
How we become capable.
How we discover just
how capable we can be.

Struggle transforms

The butterfly's cocoon

We often speak of the beauty of transformation. The butterfly emerging from its cocoon in all its glory. The cute caterpillar, going into the cocoon. Even the cocoon itself we associate with safety, a soft enveloping away from the outside world. Wrapping up in cotton wool.

And yet. 'Cut a chrysalis open, and you will find a rotting caterpillar,' writes Pat Barker, in the novel *Regeneration*, '... the process of transformation consists almost entirely of decay.'[47]

It's a thousand tiny funerals. For the things that never were, and the things that are no longer.

The letting go, of who you thought you were, or wanted to be, or who you thought you wanted to be.

Letting it burn. The scaffolding. The relics. The carefully crafted cage.

The digging out of the rot, the cutting away, the amputation. The peeling away of layers, leaving you raw and exposed.

It feels like death, because it is.

The kind of death that clears the ground and provides rich fertile soil to grow from.
The kind of death from which life emerges.

---

[47] Pat Barker, *Regeneration*, 1991.

Who we become

Scientists have a name for this: Post-traumatic growth.

It's where people emerge from a traumatic event with a stronger sense of identity, a positive shift in perspective or mindset, a deeper sense of meaning and purpose or connection to others.

Games designer Jane McGonigal describes how she discovered this when she found herself bedridden and suicidal following a severe concussion. In her TED talk she lists the top five traits of post-traumatic growth:[48]

1. My priorities have changed – I'm not afraid to do what makes me happy.
2. I feel closer to my friends and family.
3. I have a new sense of meaning and purpose.
4. I understand myself better. I know who I really am now.
5. I'm better able to focus on my goals and dreams.

These are a mirror opposite to the five regrets of the dying:

1. I wish I hadn't worked so hard.
2. I wish I had stayed in touch with my friends.
3. I wish I had let myself be happier.
4. I wish I'd had the courage to express my true self.

---

[48] Jane McGonigal, 'The game that can give you 10 extra years of life', TED talk, June 2012. Available from www.ted.com/talks/jane_mcgonigal_the_game_ that_can_give_you_10_extra_years_of_life [accessed 17 November 2020].

5. I wish I'd lived a life true to my dreams, instead of what others expected of me.

If we allow ourselves to transform, we become stronger, truer versions of ourselves.

We know ourselves better. We trust ourselves more.

We live truer lives.

Terrifically alive

In survival mode, it is safety that keeps us alive. Fear serves as a warning, a sign to steer clear and run away, or stay put and don't rock the boat.

But transformation is different. It's where being afraid and alive collide. It's where we emerge from the cage that was keeping us safe and small, sheltered and numb, guarded and captive – into the bracing, wild expanse where we feel it all. The terror and the excitement, the pain and the joy, the vulnerability and the freedom.

It's where we become terrifically alive.

I love that Brené Brown openly admits to this, that two decades of studying and teaching courage and vulnerability doesn't exempt her from feeling terrified. She writes in *The Gifts of Imperfection*,[49] and repeats in *Rising Strong*:

> One minute you'll pray that the transformation stops, and the next minute you'll pray that it never ends. You'll also wonder how you can feel so brave and so afraid at the same time. At least that's how I feel most of the time... brave, afraid and very, very alive.[50]

If it's good enough for Brené, it's good enough for me.

---

[49] Brené Brown, *The Gifts of Imperfection: Let Go of Who You Think You're Supposed to Be and Embrace Who You Are*, 2010.

[50] Brené Brown, *Rising Strong: How the Ability to Reset Transforms the Way We Live, Love, Parent, and Lead*, 2015, p. 254.

Feel it all. The terror and the excitement, the pain and the joy, the vulnerability and the freedom.

Struggle reveals

Unintended superpowers

Attached to the community centre cafe where I often meet up with my friend Josie is a range of accommodation for the elderly, people with learning disabilities and a specialist dementia care facility. Among the residents who frequent the cafe is another Josie. Most people struggle to understand her, because she mumbles, which she in turn finds frustrating and isolating.

One person who does understand her is my friend Josie. It turns out Josie's son had speech difficulties in his early years, and she had to get good at deciphering mumbling. So now, she is one of the few people able to offer this lonely woman a lifeline of connection, understanding and friendship.

It's remarkable to witness. I call it her unintended super-power. Our mutual friend Jude affectionately likens it to Han Solo and Chewbacca.

One of the unintended superpowers my husband has is that you can rarely catch him out with trick questions. Like this one:

Can you find the the **mistake**?
1 2 3 4 5 6 7 8 9

Or this one:

Quick! Count the number of times that the letter 'f' appears in the following sentence:

'Finished files are the result of years of scientific study combined with the experience of years.'

How many did you find?

Most people answer three because they overlook the word 'of'. And if you're still trying to find the mistake in the first example, point to each word in turn and read it aloud, slowly.

Because my husband is dyslexic, reading doesn't come easily to him; he's less likely to skim read, the way that I do. The technical term is disfluency.

Disfluency slows you down, but there's an advantage to that.

Nobel prize-winning psychologist Daniel Kahneman describes two thinking systems that our brains use: System 1, which is fast, intuitive, automatic and effortless; and System 2, which is slower, analytical, intentional, and takes more effort.[51] In questions like the above, System 1 comes up with the quickest answer, but System 2 is likely to come up with the more accurate answer.

Two other psychologists, Adam Alter and Daniel Oppenheimer, discovered that if you make the font of these kinds of questions harder, people switch from System 1 to System 2. Disfluency, they found, activates analytical reasoning. By making the brain work harder, people scored better.[52]

---

[51] Daniel Kahneman, *Thinking Fast and Slow*, 2011.

[52] Adam L. Alter, Daniel M. Oppenheimer, Nicholas Epley and Rebecca N. Eyre (2007). Overcoming intuition: Metacognitive difficulty activates analytic reasoning. *Journal of Experimental Psychology: General*, 136(4): 569–76.

And since my husband's brain already has to work hard to read, it's perfectly primed for the analytical reasoning that sees through the trick question.

Struggle reveals

Make the font harder to read and people score better. What do we miss when things are too easy?

One of the most valuable things we take from being in struggle is the knowledge that we can. We can struggle. We can survive. We can overcome. And often we develop skills along the way that we wouldn't have if things were easy.

Talking with a friend the other day about how to prepare our kids for university, I found myself laughing, reminiscing about all the mistakes I made, and how some of my best learning came from the times when I messed up.

The time when I turned up at Leeds train station at Christmas, with nowhere to go.
The time when I was homeless and couch-surfed for two weeks because I hadn't realized I had to reapply to stay on campus over the summer.
The time when I spent half my student loan on John Lewis bedding, then realized I needed to get a job!

It's the sort of thing that would have me crying 'Noo!' at the thought of my kids putting themselves in that sort of position. Maybe it was fortuitous that my parents had the foresight to move halfway across the world when I left home for uni, because I know for me the temptation to swoop in and intervene would be high.

But I learned so much from those days. I learned that I was resourceful. I learned to negotiate, to barter and ask for help. I learned the value of community. I learned to find answers when I didn't have them. And yes, I learned the need for planning!

So often we think we need to prepare our kids by telling them how to get it right.

Perhaps what they (and we) need to hear is: You'll get it wrong, and that's when you'll learn best.

Instead of 'don't panic' there's nothing wrong:

Don't panic. You've been here before. You can deal with this.

We can do hard things.

Beauty of not quite fitting in

In the book *David and Goliath*, Malcolm Gladwell explores the advantages of disadvantages (and the disadvantages of advantages), from a basketball team who played unconventionally to compensate for their weaknesses, to the shepherd boy David who effectively brought a gun to a knife fight, when he faced the giant Goliath.

In a chapter subtitled 'You wouldn't wish dyslexia on your child. Or would you?' he suggests that one advantage that comes with dyslexia is a familiarity with being the outsider, which might make it easier to be 'disagreeable': 'I don't mean obnoxious or unpleasant. I mean... willing to take social risks – to do things that others might disapprove of.'[53]

Makes sense, doesn't it? If you've never fitted in in the first place, you might be less invested in conforming to social norms, less worried about what other people think. Which, of course, is a highly desirable trait for innovators and change makers.

As well as dyslexia, my husband also has a certain social blindness. Where some of us might get a little starstruck or self-conscious speaking to someone very important, he'd happily speak as openly to a senior director in his company as he would anybody else in the building. Only afterwards would someone say, 'You do realize who that is right?'

---

[53] Malcolm Gladwell, *David and Goliath: Underdogs, Misfits and the Art of Battling Giants*, 2013.

As a result, he often has the ear of senior directors. Not because he charms his way up, but precisely because he doesn't sugarcoat. Equally, he chats just as openly with a cleaner, a security guard or someone with a learning disability. Because social status is not something he registers, it doesn't occur to him to treat anybody differently.

Fitting in is something I also struggled with as a child. Living between two continents, two cultures, attending seven different schools, I was often the outsider. The second-generation immigrant. The third culture kid.[54]

Nothing about me fitted. My thick glasses didn't fit my tiny nose and my big teeth. My skin colour didn't match my accent. My penchant for thick books and deep conversation didn't fit with what regular kids did for fun. My love for learning, my ignorance of popular culture and my mispronunciation of place names – none of it fit. I was a weird kid.[55]

The beauty of that now is put me in a room full of strangers and I can easily strike up a conversation. I'm blessed with a wide network of friendships, rather than one closed circle. I can turn my ear and my empathy to people with diverse perspectives, interests and experiences – a very useful skill for a coach, and arguably much needed in an increasingly polarized world.

I can also spot the opportunities that are not right for me and have a healthy allergy to no-holds-barred gung ho gurus

---

[54] A term coined in the 1950s by sociologist Ruth Hill Useem, also referred to as 'citizens of everywhere and nowhere'. See Kate Mayberry, 'Third Culture Kids: Citizens of everywhere and nowhere', BBC, 18 November 2016. Available from www.bbc.com/worklife/article/20161117-third-culture-kids-citizens-of-everywhere-and-nowhere [accessed 17 November 2020].

[55] For the record, I'm still weird now. When my friends tell me that, I take it gratefully as a compliment. It means they really know me.

selling their six-figure formula as the only way to success. Rather than think that's not the industry for me, I recognize it's just not the right approach for me.

I can pick and choose my own path, without leaving a part of me behind.

Where else would you find a naturally disorganized productivity coach? I could have easily seen that as a reason to disqualify myself. In fact, I did for a while. I resisted the field of productivity and 'time management' for a long time, precisely because I'm not one of those naturally organized types. Turns out that gives me a level of empathy, insight and understanding that my clients and readers find 'refreshingly human'.

Think about it. If you had a child who was struggling with Maths and wanted to hire a tutor, would you want to hire the Maths genius, the one who finds everything comes naturally, who can just give them the answer? Or would you want to hire the one who knows what it's like to struggle, who can actually guide your child in their learning?

As I often quote my friend Marianne Cantwell, the author of *Be a Free Range Human*, saying, 'Our weaknesses are just our strengths in the wrong environment.'

And in her brilliant TEDx talk on liminality, 'The hidden power of not (always) fitting in':[56]

It's always those pieces we're so tempted to hide in the shadows, that turn out to be our edge when we bring them into the light.

---

[56] Marianne Cantwell, 'The hidden power of not (always) fitting in', TEDx Norwich education talk, 2017. Available from www.youtube.com/watch?v=cnooCepNZv4 [accessed 17 November 2020].

Regret versus longing

I should have called.
I should have known.
I should have done/said/not said...

Regret makes the heart sick. It is a special kind of punishment we use to justify the pain that we feel. To take control and direct the anger, even if it is to ourselves.

But what that pain is trying to express is longing.

Take away the 'should' and you reveal longing.

I long for us to have spoken. I long for him to have known. I long for things to be different.

I long for the courage to speak. I long for the chance to change things.

For things to be whole. For her to be here. For him to be free. Nothing missing. Nothing broken.

Longing speaks the truth of our pain. Our anger. While releasing control.

Why does this matter?

Because regret eats us alive. When we direct all that energy inward to a past we have no power to change, it consumes us. We become impossibly demanding, of ourselves and others. We become paralysed for fear of making the wrong decision (again).

We use what power we have to beat the power out of us. It's possibly the worst kind of self-harm.

Only when we release control and acknowledge the longing for what it is – the pain that is for us to feel, not to fix. The beauty that we yearn for, not the blame to seek. That we realize just how much power we do have. In the choices that we make going forward, the creations that are birthed from our pain, the changes we pursue in seeking justice, or beauty, or freedom.

Longing becomes the fuel in which we rise from the ashes.

Struggling together

An alternative to being the fixer

In my early days of parenting I struggled. *(I still struggle now, but I struggled with struggling back then.)*

My husband would come home from work and I would pour out every detail of my day to him – from practical minutia of feeding times and nappy changes to raging emotions I couldn't make head or tail of.

His go-to response was to try and fix things. He'd move furniture round, empty the bins, do the washing up, rescue the spaghetti. But the thing he couldn't fix was how I felt. The suffocation of never having a moment to myself, at the same time as feeling inexplicably alone. The certainty of the weight of responsibility with the disorientation of not really having a clue. The joy and ache at the miracle of life, and the thousand tiny decisions I couldn't help obsess over.

What I needed then wasn't a fixer. What I was going through did not need fixing. Nor removing. Nor solving. It was the searing, blinding intensity of motherhood.

I don't need you to do it for me. I don't need you to take it away. I need to know I can do it. I need to know you know I can do it.

I need to know that you are here, that I am here, and neither of us are in the wrong place.
I need to be seen and known.

I needed a witness.

Showing up

My friend Rachel once had a team member who was being hauled into a disciplinary because she'd been off sick too much.

Rachel fundamentally disagreed with the disciplinary. This was a valuable member of her team, who was valiantly juggling the pain of being ill, the uncertainty of not knowing what the heck was wrong with her, the logistics of medical appointments, as well as doing her job brilliantly when she could. In fact, the quality of her work had not suffered, but the quantity of time spent at work had triggered this process, and the powers that be had taken it out of her hands.

There was nothing Rachel could do about it. She couldn't stop it. She could choose not to attend. She could publicly wash her hands of it, distance herself and make her protest clear: I don't agree with this. I won't be part of this. Not in my name.

But she chose to be in the room. Not because she agreed with it. But because she knew the one thing she could do was to be the one friendly face in the room for her colleague. She couldn't take this cup away from her, but she sure as heck could walk through hell with her.

Fixing versus witnessing

The fixer advises. The witness acknowledges.
The fixer shows. The witness sees.
The fixer replaces. The witness reflects.

The fixer offers sympathy, 'I feel for you.'
The witness offers compassion, 'I feel with you.'

The fixer says, 'I've got this.' The witness says, 'I'm with you, and you've got this.'

The fixer wants to take our burden. The witness gives us strength.

I'm with you. You've got this.

Scaffolding

'I'm trying to hold it all together here...'

Some of us are natural scaffolders. We're great at holding it all together. People. Teams. Projects. Families. Relationships. We hold it all together.

Scaffolding is so needed to create stability and structure, to enable repair or construction to take place. But if that repair work doesn't happen, or the foundations are missing, no amount of scaffolding can keep a building from crumbling.

Scaffolding is only ever meant to be temporary. To support the creation of something lasting.

We can make the scaffolding look beautiful from the outside, but inside is where we find true strength, health or decay.

If we're permanently in scaffold-mode, we'll always be on the outside, holding everything together, rather than living in the building and being part of what's inside.

The real change needs to happen on the inside. At the core. Within the people or the relationship we're supporting.

We get so caught up in sustaining life we forget to live that life. We forget that 'a relationship', as the writer Rebecca Solnit puts it, 'is a story you construct together and take up residence in'.[57]

---

[57] Rebecca Solnit, *A Field Guide to Getting Lost*, 2005, p. 135.

What makes you strong doesn't make me weak

Despite living only a few miles away from Cannock Chase, an Area of Outstanding Natural Beauty with its acres of woodland, heathland, trails and wildlife, including I'm told a herd of around 800 fallow deer, I am woefully unfamiliar with much of it outside of the two visitor centres.

Thankfully, I have friends who have grown up here and know every inch of it well, who sometimes take me exploring. On one such visit, my friend Christiana pointed out the birch trees, with their tall, majestic trunks, reaching ever upwards. Turns out they do this to compete for sunlight. Along the way, any side branches that get in the way of another get knocked off, leaving behind patches known as wounds.

It reminded me of Canary Wharf. The corporate jungle where bodies and buildings jostle each other, competing to rise to the top, with its promise of cleaner air and clearer skies. A world where climbing up is inextricably linked to pushing someone else down – if not deliberately, then unintentionally by blocking out their light.

When we buy into this world, we fall into the trap of comparison. We see the success of others as a threat to ourselves. We meet their strengths with suspicion, and their results with resentment. We grandstand to keep others in their place, so we don't get crowded out.

The problem is comparison kills.

It kills our creativity, shutting everything down with a critical eye – ourselves, others, ideas that are different from ours, ideas that are too similar to ours.

It steals our joy. It's hard to enjoy what we have when we're constantly looking over our shoulder at what others might have, or might take from us.

It numbs our compassion. It's bloody hard to feel for someone when we feel threatened by them.

Frankly, I don't want to be a birch. I want to be an ancient oak that sprawls and provides a home to birds and bugs, a canopy for holly and bluebells, and food for rabbits and squirrels.

Let's create a different world.
A world where we stop comparing.
A world where we all have space to grow.

What makes you strong doesn't make me weak.
What makes me strong doesn't make you weak.

When we realize that, we can celebrate each other's successes and strengthen each other in our struggles. We can be inspired by each other, contribute to each other's creativity, and let joy be our contagion.

When we stop comparing, we can all breathe freer.

And grow stronger.

**When we stop comparing,
we can all breathe freer.**

And grow stronger.

Comrades and co-conspirators

My son was very ill with Covid. I could do nothing, no visiting, no going back to Glasgow, just waiting. My team were fantastic and I have realized I can let go a bit.

Out of the nine people in my team, eight have had a family, medical or domestic emergency during lockdown. We've learned to work differently and we've supported each other through some pretty tough times.

And all of that came out of unexpected emergencies. As you can see our emergencies are like Glasgow buses – nothing for ages and then eight come at once.

> Tricia Armstrong, Chair of the British Global Travel Health Association

In these moments of crisis and struggle we discover.

We discover the truth about ourselves and our people, how much we're capable of and what really matters, when we strip away the stuff we get caught up in day to day.

We discover the beauty of teamwork and community, when we let go of trying to do everything ourselves.

Our biggest fear is that we can't do it all ourselves. But look what happens when that actually comes true.

Turns out what makes me weak, makes us strong.

Our biggest fear is that we can't do it all ourselves. But look what happens when that actually comes true.

Turns out what makes me weak, makes us strong.

Single-handed or stronger together?

So much of our culture celebrates the lone hero, the star that rises to the top, the champion, the extraordinary, the 1%.

When researching this book, it struck me how many business and entrepreneurial books are geared around the tradition of slaying the competition. In fact, one book I looked at was described as something that would help its readers become 'world-beaters'.

The myth of single-handed success is what puts us in competition with each other, and perpetuates the 'dog-eat-dog' world where success means being better than everyone else.

Personally, I'm far more interested in being a world-changer than a world-beater. And I know I'm not alone.

In 2016, the World Economic Forum's Future of Jobs study listed among its predicted top ten skills for 2020: people management, co-ordinating with others and emotional intelligence.[58]

In a 2018 interview, Minouche Shafik, director of the London School of Economics said, 'In the past jobs were about

---

[58] Melanie Curtin, 'The 10 top skills that will land you high-paying jobs by 2020, according to the World Economic Forum, Inc.' Available from www.inc.com/melanie-curtin/the-10-top-skills-that-will-land-you-high-paying-jobs-by-2020-according-to-world-economic-forum.html [accessed 17 November 2020].

muscles, now they're about brains, but in future they'll be about the heart.'[59]

And as one Forbes article on compassionate leadership put it:

> ... as global competition and heightened uncertainty
> has driven organizations to outsource, flatten and
> cut back (often quite mindlessly and heartlessly – the
> two tend to go hand in hand), people have become
> increasingly hungry for a deeper sense of meaning in
> their work and a closer connection between what they
> do and how it serves a greater good.[60]

Compassion and collaboration.

Productivity isn't just about how and what you achieve, but how you enable others to achieve – and how they enable you. It's time to focus on how we work together to make change – rather than who comes out on top.

It's time to leave the myth of single-handed success behind.

Not just in the big names that we celebrate, but also in how we value each other.

Questions like 'how does she do it all?' suggest that single-handedly coping with everything is the pinnacle of achievements. A so-called motivational quote I spotted on Facebook the other day – about how strong women were once broken girls who have learned to never depend on anyone

---

[59] Minouche Shafik interview, *Alain Elkann Interviews*. Available from www.alainelkanninterviews.com/minouche-shafik [accessed 17 November 2020].

[60] Margie Warrell, 'Compassionate leadership: A mindful call to lead from both head and heart', Forbes, 20 May 2017. Available from www.forbes.com/sites/margiewarrell/2017/05/20/compassionate-leadership/#1f28ed925df9 [accessed 17 November 2020].

– broke my heart. And we know it's not just women this affects when three quarter of all suicides are male.

What if we stopped associating strength and success with the ability to achieve things single-handedly?

One of my heroes is Paul Erdős, a Hungarian mathematician who was such a prolific collaborator that there's a number named after him, which measures your collaborative distance from the man.

In his lifetime, he co-authored papers with 500 other mathematicians, which gives them an Erdős number of 1. If you wrote a paper with one of those people, you'd have an Erdős number of 2. Over 40,000 people have an Erdős number of 3 or less.

Ok, he also took amphetamines, was known to be 'impossibly demanding' and couldn't even pack his own bags[61] – those things I don't aspire to! But imagine having contributed to that many people's work? That's an astonishing legacy.

Whose work do you contribute to? Who contributes to yours? How might your world of work change with collaboration instead of competition?

---

[61] According to Tim Harford, *Messy*, 2016.

Crowd versus community

L et's be clear: community life is messy too, and imperfect. Communities can be noisy places and people can be unpredictable. Sometimes the pain of working together can make it feel like it's easier (and more efficient) to just do it ourselves.

One reader described to me:

> Today I feel like I'm on a packed commuter train, standing with no room to move. I'm trying to edge forward but I'm getting pushed back. The only thing keeping me upright are the crowds, but it is also them who are holding me back.
>
> If the train driver applies the brakes suddenly, we are all going to end up in a heap, and with my luck I will be at the bottom!!

Such a vivid image! One that many of us can identify with in this day and age where work is relentless and life keeps getting busier, bigger, brighter, louder and faster.

The very people we live and work with can be both the people who hold us back and the people who hold us up.

We're not short on people. But are we a crowd, where everyone serves themselves? Or are we a community where we serve each other?

When we are a crowd, we end up getting in each other's way, but when we are a community, we can accomplish things and reach places that no individual can.

What are you investing in – crowd control or community building?

A note on grace

One of the things that continues to catch me by surprise in my faith is the word *grace*. You really think I'd be used to it by now.

I used to joke that my name was a contradiction in terms. I was the least graceful child you could find. All bones and angles and awkwardness.

But I do wonder if it was some cosmic joke that it's the name I was given, because it's the thing I need reminding of most often.

The thing about grace is it's not earned. It's not about how good you get or how much you give. It's all about receiving.

So many of us are so much more comfortable giving than receiving. We are far more willing to give help than admit that we need help.

Giving feels good. It's kind, it's generous, it's celebrated. It signifies success and plenty.

Receiving on the other hand feels vulnerable. It signals lack and need. It's saying I don't have enough; I need help.

No wonder the Lutheran pastor Nadia Bolz-Weber calls receiving grace 'the best shitty feeling in the world. I don't want to need it. Preferably I could just do it all and be it all and never mess up.'[62]

---

[62] Nadia Bolz-Weber, *Accidental Saints*, 2015, p. 179.

And that's the beauty of grace. Fundamentally it's the beauty of not being enough on our own. Because if we were enough on our own, we would never need anybody else. And we wouldn't have each other.

Which reminds me that relationships are two way. If I am only ever the giver, I don't get to experience the beauty of true connection. Generosity can only happen if I'm willing to receive as well as give.

That's the thing about real connection and true community. It's not about you or me. It's about what we create together.

The world of the generous

The world of the generous gets larger and larger. The world of the stingy gets smaller and smaller.

Proverbs 11:24–26, The Message

Whether we live in a community or a crowd depends on us. As a community grows, we all grow. As a crowd grows, we get pressed down.

We create a generous world when we see each other.
When we speak life rather than death, when we celebrate rather than criticize.
When we co-create rather than compare.

We create a generous world when we allow ourselves to be seen. When we are brave enough to let go of what doesn't belong or fit. When we trust enough to make space for something truer.

We create a generous world when we receive as generously as we give.
When we allow imagination and curiosity to bridge the divides of fear and uncertainty.

When we learn that our capacity for love is not merely reciprocal, contingent on the love shown to us, but rooted in something far more ancient and enduring than popularity, chemistry or fleeting emotion.

And that kind of love is contagious. The more you give, the more it spreads and multiplies, and the more you have.

New rules outside the comfort zone

New rules outside the comfort zone

Just because you're struggling doesn't mean you're failing. Signs of weakness can become your source of strength.

Resistance is where we stretch.
Getting it wrong is where we discover.

Confidence isn't about how much we know, but how comfortable we are with what we don't know.
Courage is not the absence of fear but the facing of it.

Joy, grief, peace, pain. Feel it all. You're alive.
Struggle is not the root of despair, but a source of hope.

Hope

Hope is not always happy lighthearted dreamy
feelings. On the contrary – sometimes it's a bit of a
heartbreaker... Why?

Hope is not content with the status quo.

Hope sees where the status quo leaves others broken
and lost and hurting.

Hope knows there is more... a better world, a more
just and equitable world, a healthier world than this.
Healthier people, whole relationships, a better way.

So yes, Hope weeps and grieves.

And then, Hope gets to work.

Jo Saxton[63]

'Hope is a function of struggle,' writes Brené Brown.[64] 'If we're
never allowed to fall or face adversity as children, we are
denied the opportunity to develop the tenacity and sense of
agency we need to be hopeful.'

---

[63] Jo Saxton, Instagram post, 30 July 2020. Available from www.instagram.
com/p/CDPsJkLlo4l [accessed 17 November 2020].

[64] Brené Brown, *Rising Strong: How the Ability to Reset Transforms the Way We
Live, Love, Parent, and Lead*, 2015, p. 202.

Hope isn't knowing that you have a get out of jail free card, or seeing light at the end of the tunnel, or waiting for an end to come.

It's knowing that the tunnel isn't where you stay. It's knowing you have what it takes to get up and get walking, to roll your sleeves up and get working.

When you're done, neither you nor the tunnel will be the same.

Holy shit

Not everything happens for a reason, but a reason can come out of everything.

Jenny Ainsworth[65]

Nope, shit doesn't happen for a reason. But it does happen. Like Jenny, I don't buy into some kind of God-ordained or Universe-conspired plan that plays us like pawns on a chess board.

I do however believe in hope. The kind of hope that – to borrow a phrase from singer-songwriter Bruce Cockburn – kicks at the darkness until it bleeds daylight. The kind of hope that holds onto joy with bleeding fingernails. When everything we've been taught tells us this doesn't belong here, hope says, 'Oh yes it does.'

I also believe that as human beings, we are a meaning-making species. If there's something we are intrinsically equipped to do, it is to redeem something good from what's broken, to rebuild from ground zero, to turn our stumbling blocks into stepping stones, and the stinkiest shit into rich, life-giving soil.

That's the thing about struggle. It's not some cute message about clouds and silver linings. It is hard graft. And it stinks like hell.

More often than not, we wouldn't choose it. But we can absolutely use it.

---

[65] Jenny Ainsworth, Instagram post, 29 June 2020. Available from www.instagram.com/p/CCBDuvqHTfn [accessed 17 November 2020].

Three shits

1. Oh shit...
2. What is this shit?
3. Holy shit!

First comes the recognition. Then the reckoning. Then the revelation.

It may not happen all at once. There can be days, weeks, even years in between. However long it takes, it's well worth it.

Struggle is not a sign of failure, a bad omen or a wrong turn. It is not a battle to face down, a trap to be avoided or an enemy to be destroyed.

Struggle is the wilderness in which we discover.
The catalyst by which we stretch, strengthen and rise.
The birthplace of really good work, and the meeting place of community.

When you find yourself in one of life's shittier moments, don't panic, don't despair.

Take a deep breath and dig in.
You're in good company.

Acknowledgements

Writing this book has been the best kind of struggle, and I couldn't have done it without the wit, wisdom and belief of so many fellow travellers.

The conversation that started it all was with Karen Skidmore the evening after I managed to escape Waterloo station. It continued over coffee the next morning on the way to Alison Jones' writing day, and culminated in four fateful words over lunch: 'yes, it's got legs...'

Alison Jones deserves special mention for her unwavering support, enthusiasm and generally not letting me off the hook on getting this book written – and written well. Her team at Practical Inspiration Publishing are a joy to work with – and I must say, they put up with my many 'but what do you think?' messages with good grace and humour.

To everyone who burst out laughing when I told them the title – you have no idea how much that encouraged me. Jude, Julie, Chris, Al and Ashley, thank you for your early support of this project. I know I didn't have much to show in those early days, but it all helped. And to all the wonderful humans who have shared their stories with me along the way, I treasure our conversations.

Massive thanks to my beta readers Helen Frewin, Richard Tubb, Tricia Armstrong, Graham Allcott, Bec Evans, Ange Disbury, Jenny Ainsworth, Josie George and Sean Sankey for challenging me on my blindspots and the phrases that only make sense in my head. Your generous candour and encouragement is the best kind of grit – and any awkward words that remain are entirely down to my own stubbornness.

As always, my deepest love and appreciation goes to my family, Grante, Oliver and Catherine, who graciously put up with having an extrovert wife and mother who (over)shares for a living. I love you. And sorry that you probably can't take this one into school for World Book Day!

And finally to you, dear reader. A fellow author once told me that each reading is an act of co-creation. I may have provided the words, but your imagination created something unique with it. I'd love to continue the conversation. Come on over and say hello at GraceMarshall.com.

About the author

Award-winning author Grace Marshall is known for her 'refreshingly human' approach to productivity.

Her first book, *21 Ways to Manage the Stuff that Sucks Up Your Time*, was hailed by readers as the ideal book for people who don't have time to read a time management book. Her second book, *How to be Really Productive*, won the Commuter's Read category at the CMI 2017 Management Book of the Year Awards.

Her work as a Productivity Ninja with global productivity training company, Think Productive, has taken her from Norway to New York, with stages ranging from corporate headquarters to a tent in the New Forest, helping thousands of people adopt new ways of working, replacing stress, overwhelm and frustration with success, sanity and satisfaction.

Her practical advice on productivity and work-life balance has been featured in *The Guardian*, Forbes, HuffPost, CNN, London Economic Forum, Cityparents and on BBC radio.

She lives in Stafford in the middle of the UK with her husband and two kids, continually working on being a good-enough mum most of the time, with intermittent lapses into hopelessness and brilliance.